Now that I'm thinking about it...

Selected writings of
Densley Harley Palmer
2009 to 2015

© Densley Harley Palmer 2015

Published by Cave Art Press, Anacortes, WA 98221
An imprint of Douglass, Hemingway & Co., LLC
CaveArtPress.com

Cave
Art
Press

ISBN 9781934199183

These writings have all appeared previously in unpublished collections. My thanks go to Réanne Hemingway-Douglass and Arlene Cook of Cave Art Press for their encouragement to assemble them for wider publication and for Arlene's expertise in taking on the task of turning my manuscript into a book. Such a possibility had crossed my mind for many years, but it took knowledgeable friends to work the magic necessary to bring it about. They have my deepest appreciation.

Book design and cover photograph by Arlene Cook.

To Joyce Eileen Fields Palmer
Loving wife and life partner for over five decades

CONTENTS

From 2009   1

From *Whittlin'* 2009-2010   25

From *And did I tell you* 2009-2011   79

From *Legacy* 2011-2012   137

From *Pieces of my Mind* 2013-2014   203

From *And around we go* 2014-2015   241

Alphabetical list of poems   262

About the author   270

From 2009

Changing of the guard

It knows.
My old Penguin Rhyming Dictionary
knows it is being put out to pasture.
Dog-eared, coffee stained,
and, for reasons I do not recall,
at entry **261-erl**
pages have forsaken their attachment to the binding.

My old companion has offered up
its final list of rhyming possibilities
for my tortured verse.

A new dictionary, pocket-sized no less,
came as a 2008 Christmas gift from daughter Diana.
More compact, round at the corners,
it has yet to start molting pages, or
exhibit embarrassing coffee rings.

I have pondered how many uses
paper-backed dictionaries are designed to withstand
before they begin to molt pages,
as has happened to my last three.
Perhaps the fault is mine
for not being able to rhyme from memory:
needing now to rely more and more
on external assistance.

It will be difficult to jettison my old,
purple and white-covered edition;
we have shared so much time,

so many cups of sloshed coffee,
so many non-rhyming words together.

I wonder if even now my old dictionary is
looking up a rhyme for abandoned?

Conundrum

I dare not worship what I name
lest it my idol be.
Nor should I my revered describe,
lest it resemble me.

I'm giv'n to bind those things I name
with language as my knot
and seem unable to take in
that which is no-thing: not.

I'm prone to think my images
reveal how all must be
and tend to hold my symbols up
as if reality.

Alas, poor creature that I am
to such conundrum meet;
for every idol I revere
must rest on clayish feet.

Hymn tune: *Ellacombe*

Come together sing of oneness

Great and small dwell in communion,
seen and unseen live and grow.
Should we sunder these connections,
all life will a rupture know.
Sing in praise of all in union
part to part united, whole.
Lift aloud a grand thanksgiving
as we share in common soul.

We cannot detect the blending
that exists through all that lives.
Life to life in one great fullness,
each with each together thrives.
Sing in praise of all in union
part to part united, whole.
Lift aloud a grand thanksgiving
as we share in common soul.

Who are we to rend a wholeness
in which no part stands alone?
Ours it is to view it fully
linked together, joined in one.
Sing in praise of all in union
part to part united, whole.
Lift aloud a grand thanksgiving
as we share in common soul.

Come together, sing our oneness
that each in this moment knows.
Lift a song of grateful wonder
for each life the sacred sows.

Sing in praise of all in union
part to part united, whole.
Lift aloud a grand thanksgiving
as we share in common soul.

Hymn text: *Hymn to joy*

We dwell at the margin of shore, sea, and sky

A hymn for Earth Day 2009

We dwell at the margin of shore, sea, and sky
on whose fragile balance all living rely.
A symmetry wondrous not ours to molest
but ours to pass forward as nature's bequest.

The oceans of earth served as womb for all life;
their depths teem with creatures and mysteries rife.
Yet she spreads her substance abroad o'er the earth
in raincloud, as snowflake to give each brook birth.

We must not view rain drop, ripe field or fresh stream
without seeing oceans as whole, without seam.
Seas yield up a bounty in which all life shares,
thus to us falls duty to honor her care.

Hymn text: *St. Denio*

Dancing

Joyce and I have seldom danced together
in the nearly 50 years of our marriage;
I mean the kind of dancing where people
dress up and go to a hall or ballroom
where a band plays on a stage
and other people can identify your partner
from your proximity to one another.

We've talked on and off
about taking dance lessons
since both of us danced one way or another
many years ago before we became a set.

We mostly danced with our children
when we were all younger.
The kind of jumping, twirling and handholding
that makes children and their parents
grow dizzy and giggle,
sometimes ending with everyone
falling on the floor in a laughing, quaking heap.

There were times
when our daughters stood on my toes
as we danced our way around the living room.
I don't recall son Clark ever doing that with me.

Sometimes, as we wound our way along grocery aisles,
I added a fancy step or two to our march
to interrupt the tedium of shopping
but mostly to see how the kids would react.
Predictably, they lamented my efforts at grace
and made it clear I was embarrassing them.

I still dance across the room when we are home
trying to fit my less-than-coordinated movements
to melodies playing in my head or on television.
But you'd think we were in the grocery store aisle again
the way the granddaughters roll their eyes
and snort "Oh, grandpa."

It's then I know I've still got it!

I would pluck splinters from your eyes

I would pluck splinters from your eyes
but a dark copse in my own
blinds my vision.

You are but a blur
shaped,
obscured by the scales
through which I would see.

Oh, that I could see in you
beyond a reflection of myself.

Perhaps then I would perceive
there are no splinters
in your eyes at all.

Here it is again

Here it is again:
a blank screen with an annoyingly
incessant cursor blinking
in the upper left corner.

True, it would not be here
had I not pressed a button
that knows nothing better,
nothing other,
than to bring up a new screen.

"So," I wonder, "why I have called this meeting?"
What is it I have to say,
even to a blank computer screen,
that warrants taking time
from either of our days?

I don't know what it might have on its agenda,
but my head is jammed with inchoate thoughts
insisting on expression,
finding an avenue of release to see what,
if anything, they mean.

These are the thoughts that creak like
an old house on a dark windy night
causing a body to wonder who else is here.

These are the thoughts
that surge nearly to the front of one's mind
only to ebb into a hopeless stew of glop
if not given their due.

They are the thoughts that seem so bright,
so inventive, so worthy of expression,
they threaten to boil over the side of the kettle
before you toss in the pasta or beans
or whatever else it is
for which you put on the water to boil.

They are the thoughts that come
with an unexplained sense of childish urgency,
as if yelling in a descending scale, "M-a-w-m,"
only to be followed by,
"I just wondered where you were."
The screen waits mutely,
leaving to me the burden for any conversation we are
destined to have

"You called?" it inquires haughtily
as if annoyed at having been awakened
from wherever it reposes
in the dark recesses of gigamemory,
sneering as if it surely had been about something
far more important than communicating with me.

"I just wondered where you were," I answer.

How shall I sing when words won't come

How shall I sing when words won't come;
when shadows fill my bein'?
How can I sing with ears hard-stopped
and scales obscure my seein'?
There is a song I long to sing;
I feel it in me movin'.
'twould be a song of thankfulness
that grows from out my lovin'.

Words turn to dust upon my tongue;
they vanish in their sayin'.
I lift my voice to sing my song
but end up only brayin'.
There is a song I long to sing;
I feel it in me movin'.
'twould be a song of thankfulness
that grows from out my lovin'.

Perhaps it's not that I should sing,
should send my voice a ringin'
but should instead let song sing me
to set my spirit wingin'.
There is a song I long to sing;
I feel it in me movin'.
'twould be a song of thankfulness
that grows from out my lovin'.

Tune: *Endless song*

I lift a song with all about me

I lift a song with all about me,
joining in hymn of praise as one,
knowing each sings from diff'ring station:
from myriad strains, our song is spun.
Diff'ring in flesh yet one in soul,
each seeks to be complete, be whole.

May I each day move on my journey
offering gifts of trust and hope
as all together through life's turnings
drink deeply from life's common cup.
Diff'ring in flesh yet one in soul,
each seeks to be complete, be whole.

I lift my song with all about me
thankful I do not sing alone.
For in each voice, I hear fresh wisdom
born of a knowledge past my own.
Diff'ring in flesh yet one in soul,
each seeks to be complete, be whole.

Lift up your song in chorus praising
that which enlivens all that dwell
across earth's face in mix amazing,
surpassing what one voice can tell.
Diff'ring in flesh yet one in soul,
each seeks to be complete, be whole.

Hymn tune: *Neumark*

Knowing our place

We do not spread the night sky
and fill it with flaming flares,
or cause a rising sun
to bring a golden glory to the horizon
as earth turns toward what we call east.

The wind does not blow or change direction
at our command,
nor do seasons turn because of our bidding.

Is it that we are less significant
in the grand scheme of things
than we are willing to acknowledge?

Or does whatever significance
we dare claim for ourselves
arise from understanding
that all these activities
are carried on by the earth and cosmos
because of what they are
rather than because of who we are?

Life song

What if,
when our mothers carried
us in their bellies
they retired with other women
to a place outside the village
to meditate and pray
until there came to them
the song that would be ours
forever?

A song that would be sung at our birth,
our coming of age,
our marriage,
our death.

A song crooned
to sing us back to our path
when we have gone astray.

A song that would be
not only on our lips and
running through our heads
but woven as a thread
through the fabric of our being.

With appreciation to The Reverend Barbara Gilday

Porches

I have a fondness for houses with porches,
some folk call them verandas,
that stretch clear across the front of the house
and wrap down the sides
toward the back yard,
that some folk call the garden.

Many porches are partially concealed by trellises
on which climb wandering rose bushes or
grand-blossomed purple clematis,
lending an illusion of privacy to
those using the porch in the evening
or on a warm afternoon.

There is usually something like a pair of wicker rockers
or a canvas-topped three-person swing on these porches
that accommodates sitting, swinging,
some folk call it gliding,
conversation, spooning,
some folk call it canoodling,
star gazing, and even proposing a marriage
on a starry, moonlit night.

Porches are outdoor parlors,
some call them sitting rooms.
They invite passers by to call out,
maybe even stop and prop a foot
on the lowest step,
or climb right up to sit for a spell.

"Glassa lemonade? It's mighty warm today."
"Cuppa tea? Fall is coming early this year."

We lost a generation of conviviality,
some call it neighborliness,
when the generous front porch
shrunk to the size of a postage stamp
hardly enough to shelter a package
left by UPS or accommodate
a duo of uniformed little girls
purveying cookies or mints.

Porches have shrunk so much
that a band of trick-or-treaters
needs to stretch single file along our walk
and pass back treats hand to hand
to the smallest, appropriately dressed goblin
nearly unseen at the end of the line.

The back yard,
again a garden for some,
became a family's private domain,
especially when it was surrounded
by a solid wood fence even a six-footer
couldn't spy over without help of an accomplice.
Privacy won out over hospitality.

I'm glad to see generously-sized porches
are coming back. People can again sit on them
to rock, snooze, propose, watch the world pass by.

Perhaps neighborliness will come back, too.
If folk don't come right up the walk
to sit for a spell,
they may be moved to call out a greeting.
They might even call us by name.

Swaddling sacredness

What bounds do we on sacred set
as we around it trace
by image, word and ritual
constraints of time and space?

So giv'n are we to create form
in all that we perceive,
we shape perceptions to accord
with that we would believe.

It's not a fault that we are thus;
the fault's when we maintain
that what we see and what we think
can sacredness contain.

Can we conceive the limitless
with minds to limits tuned,
or shall we be content with just
a sacredness cartooned?

To S

The following grew out of a brief conversation with a woman awaiting infusion treatment at Island Hospital's oncology department. She contrasted the warm, supportive care she receives here with that she witnessed for her daughter at another cancer center.

Do they want to talk with me?
Remember my name? Offer a smile?
Even just be with me?

Or, do they see me, as well as my condition,
as terminal, apt to claim me too soon
to see me as myself,
the person I have always been?

That being a chemo patient
is a recent aberration
in the trajectory of my life?

If I have ever needed a sense of oneness
with another, surely it is now.
Now, as I sense the balance of my days
shrinking and the chance for engagement
with anyone lost forever.

I do not ask for smothering embraces:
just an acknowledging smile,
a warm touch on my hand or shoulder.
I do not seek a relationship
but a caring awareness of my existence
in this moment.

This is my now, for whatever remains of it.
I invite you to share in it
   with me.

This is your now, for whatever remains of it.
I invite you to let me share in it
   with you.

On wisdom

A sacred wisdom would abide
above, beneath, within, beside
the heart and mind of each who seeks
to learn the ways in which she speaks.

We would be wise but patience lack
to follow wisdom's cryptic track,
preferring rather to accede
to facile wit and pious creed.

Yet wisdom grows, matures, extends
herself as she her pathway wends.
'Tis wisdom who brooks no conceit
that she will e'er be whole, complete.

Though I no longer walk among you

Though I no longer walk among you,
I did not take life with me.
Life remains with you,
   with all the earth.

It was my gift
to share a time with you,
to be part of life's
intricately sculpted beauty:
   to know its exquisite fragility.

Though I no longer walk among you,
life continues on a course set for it
in the simmering, shimmering stew
   of creation's freshly-fashioned first ingredients.

My wish, my deepest hope,
is that I left for you
life more abundant,
more complete
   than had I never been.

If there are tears,
let them be for what is yet to come:
for the delights,
the moments of aching beauty
   you will yet know.

We sing of a Presence beyond human ken

We sing of a Presence beyond human ken,
a Presence surrounding, a Presence within
all creatures, all features of this planet born.
We sing of a Presence complete, unadorned.

We can't name its wonder, nor measure its scope,
this Presence, this myst'ry, this source of our hope.
Beyond our construction, beyond our intent,
the Presence awaits us as whole, never rent.

The Presence awaits us, e'en beckons us forth
to dwell in its wholeness, discover full worth.
As dearly loved children, we walk through our night
relying on Presence to grant us its light.

Hymn tune: *St. Denio*

Where do I take this faith I claim

The stimulus for this poem came from a sermon delivered by The Reverend Sally Balmer at Pilgrim Congregational UCC, Anacortes, Washington, on February 22, 2009.

Where do I take this faith I claim;
where does my faith take me?
Into the valley shadowed, still,
to heights where life blows free?

Must I protect my faith from threats:
from that which might assail,
or does my faith claim its own strength,
sustaining should I fail?

May my faith not be talisman
divining good and ill,
for bane and blessing enter life:
have done, and always will.

My faith is not meant to be leashed,
not to be tethered short,
for it must range beyond myself;
faith must with life consort.

Where shall we sacred search today

Where shall we sacred search today,
and where will she be seeking
to be made known through all the earth,
in myriad voices speaking?
We seek for that which quests for us
that we might dwell in wonder:
existing in a unity
that none can wrench asunder.

In foreign tongues, in those we know,
the sacred lifts her wonders
as she sounds in the child's sweet laugh
or 'gainst the sea cliff thunders.
With bent to see what we expect
we miss out on the glory
that dwells behind, beneath, within;
we fail to learn her story.

Our search may lead to mountain top
or to a garden laden
with sacred kiss on every bloom:
a recreated Eden.
Our quest commences in the heart
as with each pulse it beckons
the life it serves to be complete:
its course by wonder reckoned.

Hymn tune: *Endless song*

2009

From *Whittlin'* 2009-2010

And God divided light from darkness

Although it comes as it has done for billions of years
through earth turning on its axis,
there still is a marvelous freshness to each new day.
No clear demarcation of time except that which we assign it,
the night-day-night cycle lends rhythm to life.

At least it used to,
before Edison and others stayed up long hours
developing an incandescent bulb
so they could sweep aside
their candles and kerosene lanterns
to invent new generations of
gadgets to illuminate their worlds
and ours.

Their efforts surpassed even more than fire
the primordial distinction between light and dark,
activity and rest.

Were we at this moment in orbit around earth,
we would see earth flood gradually into the light of day,
ebb just as gradually into shadowed night
across continent after continent, sea after sea.

We would behold vast regions of earth wrapped
in total blackness,
others, bathed in a wash of light,
peopled by millions fighting sleep
to remain alert 24/7, 365 days a year,
as they take perverse pride in their pronouncement
"We never close."

Attending to final details

She moves without apparent direction or goal
picking up one thing, then another,
fingering it, examining it,
pressing it to her breast,
sometimes to her nose
as if to draw from it
a familiar yet now absent essence,
before restoring it to its place.

Most of this must go somewhere
but there are some,
perhaps a great many,
that will remain as cairns constructed of the past
by which to mark her path
into the future.

Which,
how many
will it take to keep memory from fading
into the wash of time?
Which will preserve a sense of connectedness
that has been forever severed?

From closet
to dresser
to nightstand
to bathroom cabinet
she shuffles, shivers,
draws her gown closer about her,
lifting, turning, sniffing, setting down
not ready to decide,

not needing to decide,
anything
yet.

Brass rings

I never did catch a brass ring
while riding a merry-go-round.
I can't even remember
riding a merry-go-round
with a brass ring to catch.

Was the ring at hand and I didn't see it,
or did I always ride on
ring-challenged machines?

Metaphors abound in this:
metaphors that even at age 73
I am not ready to consider
beyond admitting I always try
to carry a few brass rings in my pocket
wherever I go now.

A fellow just never knows
when he might run into someone
in need of a brass ring.

Each new morning is but moment

On the breeze of fresh-born morning
drift the fragrances of earth,
warmed as she spins ever sunward,
off'rings for the new day's birth.
Let us sing to bid day welcome
even though her stay be brief.
Welcome all things in their turning;
change is cast as life's motif.

Earth's own shadow sheds its darkness,
creatures wake as others sleep.
Leaning as she runs her orbit,
seasons yearly cycles keep.
Let us sing to bid day welcome
even though her stay be brief.
Welcome all things in their turning;
change is cast as life's motif.

Voyaging the realm of monsters
on a grain giv'n birth through fire,
we would view ourselves transcendent:
spawn of ash from primal pyre.
Let us sing to bid day welcome
even though her stay be brief.
Welcome all things in their turning;
change is cast as life's motif.

Each new morning is but moment
in a timeless stream of days:
fresh yet ancient, history's witness,
gift to us from stellar blaze.

Let us sing to bid day welcome
even though her stay be brief.
Welcome all things in their turning;
change is cast as life's motif.

Hymn tune: *Promise*

Fire song

From the fire rubble below
rises a man's voice
   singing.

Singing?

Singing in this residential graveyard
where blackened,
broken foundations and chimneys
stand mutely as headstones
for what once were homes?

Yet, is there no place,
including this,
that cannot be improved upon
   by song?

2009 Santa Barbara, California, Jesusita fire damage

Easter 2010

Each morn brings resurrection
from all that would constrain
our hearts, our minds, our spirits
from what they might attain.
We are set loose from bondage,
set free from shadow's blight.
From out self-darkened prisons,
we step into God's light.

It is not death which binds us
but tethers we devise
for heart, for mind, for spirit,
as blinders for our eyes.
Like colts, we're born to gambol,
like eagles, currents soar.
We sin against our birthrights
when we our lives deplore.

Each moment brings new rising
as from us stones are cast.
Each moment is new birthing,
unfettered by the past.
Let us in exultation
sing psalms of life renewed
that we might rise each morning
with freshened life imbued.

Suggested tune: *Lancashire*

Gestalt

Staring at the page,
I saw only patches of whiteness
crisscrossed by unconnected lines.

>"I don't see anything."
>"Keep looking," I heard.

I kept looking;
neither lines nor spaces
combined to become anything.

>"I still don't see...anything," I complained again.
>"Perhaps you will if you keep looking."

It was only after steady gazing
a swan appeared,
its wings spread,
its head and long, arched neck leading the way,
its body a splash of brilliant whiteness
against the black surround.

>"I can see it," I shouted.
>"Yes, I thought you would.
>Now, you always will."

Hubble

The Hubble telescope,
complex artificial eye orbiting earth,
serves up images of what humanity
has never before seen:
galaxies dating back 13 billion years
pressing back
into the beginning of a cosmos
still in the throes of its birth.

Does our pressing grow solely
from our curiosity?
Is our need to know
inherent in our DNA?

And, even if we know what happened
over 13 billion years ago,
even at the beginning of beginnings,
will it make a difference
in how we treat this home
we have so badly damaged
during our short occupancy?

Perhaps if we positioned Hubble
to aim its eye on earth…
or is the prospect of what such a view might reveal
too daunting?

Justa cuppa coffee

Coffee is meant to be sipped.
Sipped from a hard-sided, ceramic cup:
a mug if you prefer.
Coffee is meant to be hot,
slurped whole-face-on, not timidly
through a microscopic hole
pierced through a plastic-topped Styrofoam container
no matter in how many sizes it might come.

It's a "cup" of coffee, not a tall, grande, reservoir,
kidney buster or whatever other serving is proffered
by those enduring the title "barista".

Justa cuppa coffee, please.

You know, the kind Eve brewed fresh for Adam
under the Tree of the Knowledge of Good and Evil
as she served it with crisp, fresh slices
of a newly-discovered fruit she called ap-ple.

Or, the kind that kept Noah and his quartermaster
awake as they strained to see landmarks
(we're told there were none)
through a raging storm that lasted nearly six weeks.

That's all:
rich, thick, black coffee.
The kind Mary of Magdala might have offered
her guests as they reclined
after a hand-to-mouth dinner
(right hand only, of course).

Should this really be so hard?
Will I ever be able to walk into a shop
and order a cup of coffee
without being quizzed through a menu of options
that have no meaning for me?

Brewed. Small. Caffeinated. No room for cream.
That's as far as I intend to go.

Kenosis

Life requires emptying and refilling
in unbroken cycle.

Without exhaling, I cannot
experience the inflowing of new breath.

So it seems also with my spirit.

Kenosis (Greek): Emptying

Learning my place

Slow learner that I am,
creatures about me must grow weary
over how long it takes me to understand
what they would teach.

Their lessons first need to penetrate
my tightly-held delusion of innate human superiority
over all things lacking sagacity to be human:
to be like me.

It is consoling that those creatures
who would teach me
do not capriciously banish me from their classroom
like an errant third grader
to some dark, echoing hallway
where my assignment is to ponder
my academic delinquency in solitude.

Perhaps a new Copernicus will emerge,
one who will locate humanity,
not at the center or apex of life on earth,
   let alone the cosmos,
but on some peripheral node
where we can do least further damage.

With thanks to Mary Oliver for her poem, The teachers.

Memorial

Flags again fly at half staff.
Another young combatant
in one of our wars is dead,
a sacrifice to Ares,
to the conflated national gods of
Security and Pride.

How morbidly ironic
that there is greater life
in the dancing flag
than in the person it symbolizes,
for the fallen one
does not see the flag,
feel the breeze moving it,
even know his or her own death.

That dreadful awareness
is left to those who loved,
who will forever move
in the shadow of loss,
who carry the burden
of what might have been;
who will, at least for a time,
know the freshening feel
of the wind.

Morning coffee

Today, I drank my morning coffee
from a brown ceramic mug
that used to sit on a shelf
in mom and dad's kitchen.

Joyce and I remember these mugs
when we visited the folks in Portland.
The set passed on to us
when we helped clean out the house
following dad's death in the mid-1990's.

This cup is neither as large nor as heavy
as the mug I usually fill for morning coffee.
Still, it's just the right size for someone
who's supposed to be careful
about the amount of caffeine
he pours into himself each day.

I take pleasure thinking of mom and dad
enjoying a morning cup of coffee
at the privacy of their kitchen table
or seated in their familiar places in the living room.
Sometimes, I forget they had a life together
apart from us: from me.

The significance of their shared life
hit heavily with mom's death in 1989
and the months of grieving
through which the family accompanied dad
and one another. Among the losses for dad
was loss of his best friend,

beloved partner for over sixty years, and
morning coffee companion.

A lot of good memories can attach to a cup of coffee.
It's a matter of sipping slowly,
talking honestly and, once in a while,
offering to get up and fetch refills.

Eddies

The fall wind eddies in front of our garage door
sweeping golden leaves and pine needles
into a tidy, round pile on the drive.

Sometimes, life's eddies whirl us
in winding tedium
from which we try to escape.

Eddies of living can swell into maelstroms
that threaten to drown us in their swirling
currents.

No semblance of neat piles then.

Morning comes naked

Morning comes naked,
unencumbered by yesterday,
eager to be clad
in what the new day holds.

She arrives,
comfortable in her nakedness,
for this is the way she has appeared
since the first morning
of the first day.

Morning is not always well received;
some view her arrival
as portending more of the same old turmoil
and would wrap herself in the same pain,
the same hand-me-down malaise
that burdened their lives
when yesterday took leave.

Still,
morning comes,
offering herself,
her freshness to all who live
and yearn for a better today.

Of moments

They have all fled.

They must have,
for they are no longer here:
those moments cobbled together
to shape the life of the boy,
lad, old man
wrapped loosely together
in dimming memory.

Their arrival,
their departure escaped notice.

No warm embrace welcomed each one
or tearful farewell saw it off
to wherever used moments pass.

This moment,
  this now
is all that is left
for as long as it deigns to remain.

Pockets

Pockets in a feller's trousers are both
bane and blessing,
serving as a repository,
short or long term,
for a hodgepodge of treasures
collected over the course of a day or week,
sometimes even a lifetime.

Pockets provide the shy, unpracticed admirer
a place to stuff his thumbs
as the toe of a worn tennis shoe
draws an arc in the dust
while he gazes upon
the most beautiful person in the world.

A pocket can serve as a time capsule
when it holds a 60-year old scout knife,
a lucky stone rubbed smooth as satin
from frequent use,
or a cracked, but still serviceable,
stained leather wallet
that came as a gift from one of the kids.

Packed chockablock,
pockets can make a man's pants too heavy,
and cause them to slide
unceremoniously to half staff or
even to the hapless wearer's ankles.

Though I'm not saying exactly why, mind you,
I've taken to wearing suspenders.

Sacredness beyond illusion

A hymn for Advent 2009

I express appreciation to the late John C. Meagher for the ideas about imagination and illusion in relation to God in The truing of Christianity: Visions of the life and thought for the future. *Doubleday, 1990.*

Sacredness beyond illusion,
uncontained by prophet's dream;
singleness in scope and nature,
oneness running without seam.
All is holy incarnation,
born of earth, the dust of star.
Sacred breath blows unabated,
nothing shall its course deter.

Sacredness beyond illusion
which the mortal wit might hold
of that which has no dimension:
that which no thought can enfold.
All is holy incarnation,
born of earth, the dust of star.
Sacred breath blows unabated,
nothing shall its course deter.

Can we not embrace a mystery
that is not for us to solve
even as we live a history
through which sacredness evolves?

All is holy incarnation,
born of earth, the dust of star.
Sacred breath blows unabated,
nothing shall its course deter.

Hymn tune: *Promise*

A glorious morning breaks anew

A glorious morning breaks anew
embracing all with light,
restoring sight to sleep-filled eyes
held captive by the night.

Beholding new the gifts life holds
is blessing beyond worth,
for every day creates anew
a fulsome, vibrant earth.

The glorious morning breaks afresh
with off'rings newly born
to celebrate the day she brings:
adventures bright, unworn.

Hymn Tune: *St. Anne*

Somewhere a bell is ringing

Somewhere, a bell is ringing.
The kind of bell one might hear pealing
across deep valleys on snowy days
echoing,
      echoing,
           echoing
as sound retraces its path
  again and again.

The kind of bell rung by a frayed, hempen rope
that snakes through a hole from the belfry
to a lower room where the ringer grasps it to
reach and pull,
      reach and pull,
           reach and pull.

A bell usually doesn't ring
with the first haul on the rope
but only after one or two pulls
to get it swinging.
Then, it blends into a union of rhythm between
bell and ringer,
      bell and ringer,
           bell and ringer.

When I was young,
a group of us used New Year's Eve
as excuse to climb the rickety stairs and wooden ladder
to the belfry of our old church and,
at the stroke of midnight,
ring the bell hands-on by rocking its wheel

back and forth,
       back and forth,
              back and forth
as its voice rang fortissimo in our ears.

The sound was so loud
it must have carried clear across Portland
on the cold, winter air.

Stream

I stoop to seize the spilling current in my hands,
but it runs too quickly, too cold
to be captured by my stiff fingers.

It is too fast, too expert
at running its course
to be hindered by the likes of me.

Stream's destiny is to flow free,
somersault over itself,
spill noisily around whatever
dares intrude on its course,
flow as if its purpose
is to drain the whole earth.

Imagine stream's surprise on reaching the sea
to be told it must return to the mountain
  and try again.

When we work for justice

When we work for justice,
we must be open
to diminishing what we prize
so that those with little or none
may have more.

When we work for justice,
we must be willing to place
into the pot of what is to be negotiated
that which we hold dear:
that which we may even clasp closely
as part of our identify.

When we work for justice,
we must be willing not just to look at those
who have more than we have
as the source for eliminating inequity,
but at ourselves as well.

When we work for justice,
we must be open to the possibility
that we will walk away from the table
with less than we carried in.

There be dragons

There be dragons.
Everybody knows there's always been dragons.
You'd be a fool to go where dragons are.
Not enough gold in the world
could tempt a person with good sense
to go right up against a dragon
even with the strongest, sharpest sword
that's ever been forged.

Nope, I ain't seen no dragons. Don't need to.
Still, I know they're there with two ugly heads,
scales, long pointy snouts and thrashing tails.
My daddy, and his daddy before him,
told me about dragons. Daddy's brother went
to where the dragons live. Never came back.
Dragons must of ate him, I expect.

Somewhere around here
I got a map stuck away
that shows where dragons are.
Fierce-looking dragons
with all that fire and smoke belching
out of their snouts.
You can see dragons in the corners and
around the edges of any good map,
and sticking their heads up from the sea.

Been said that those there dragons
eat people what get too close
to whatever they're protecting. I don't know
what they're protecting. Don't need to.

Been told that's what dragons do
and that's good enough for me.

No need to tempt fate, I always say.
Stay away from dragons.
Far, far away.

Maybe you want
to copy my map for your kids.
So they'll stay safe, you know.

A single candle

When a single candle gutters out,
the world grows darker.

How much more is this true
when a thousand, ten thousand
are wantonly snuffed
in a convulsion of barbarity?

Perhaps losing our distrust of darkness
was not really a sign of human progress
to boast about.

Whittlin'

I'm a whittler.
Not a whittler of wood or soap:
certainly not a sculptor in stone.

I whittle ideas
like freedom, peace, justice
hatred, love, God,
eternity.
I try to whittle them into shapes
I can get my mind around.

I run into folk who testify
to understanding such ideas completely.
After only a few words,
I know they are whittlers, too, but
just don't know it yet.

As a self-confessed whittler,
I have another confession to make.
Sometimes, I forget that
what I end up with
after whittlin' for a spell,
   even for a lifetime,
isn't the whole thing.
A whale of a lot covers the floor
around where I sit:
likely a lot that's important.

Maybe it's okay to be a whittler
so long as I am honest
about what I end up with.

From experience,
it seldom turns out to be anything
I'd stake my life on,
let alone anyone else's.

We drink of common water

We drink of common water.
Water as sea
turned cloud,
turned mountain stream.

Water running on the earth,
through the earth,
collected in subterranean vaults.

Although we assert rights to water,
water is of the earth,
belongs to the earth and all
who dwell on it.
It is not ours to squander or foul:
not to claim as our own.

We must remember
all drink downstream
   from someone.

Beach leavings

A child's pail lies partially buried in the sand,
its once brightly-painted exterior faded,
encrusted by accretions of time and
labors of the sea.

Its handle barely intact,
the pail harbors
a rust-gnawed hole in the bottom.
Shells and agates it might once have held
have been long since spilled
by hand and tide.

If there ever was a small
brightly-colored shovel
serving as bucket's companion,
the relationship ended long ago,
both always wondering what became of the other.

I bend to remove it from the sand
but pause.
Might a child happen along today,
one whose pail hid at home
in the rush to leave for an outing,
one who needs just the right container
for storing a day's treasures?

Sacred Space

Pilgrimage, hajj, spiritual journey
remind of the importance
of sacred space in our lives.

Journeys toward a spiritual center,
a spiritual home
serve as imperative for the faithful.

Temples, mosques, church buildings,
settings for teaching, sacrifice, worship,
call the pilgrim back again and again.

Buildings decay, fall,
yield to earthquake, wind, fire,
assault.

Places and prophets come and pass.
Icon, ritual, liturgy
fade, change with time and disuse.

Only sacredness past sacredness,
the still small voice of the holy
      stretches beyond forever.

Walking life

We begin,
not knowing the course or length of our walks.
Something we soon learn
is that we will share them with other walkers:
many for a short distance,
some for life's entire length.

We grieve loss of those
with whom we have shared the path,
for they helped set our course,
guided through dark passages,
encouraged when our energy flagged,
laughed at their own missteps,
helped us laugh at our own.

We know our walks end
as all things end;
this is the cost exacted
for having lived.

Gestation

Of what benefit is a faith
that will not
welcome new seed,
swell with new life growing within it,
give birth to newness time
    after time
        after time?

We come in our diversity

This hymn is based on the vision statement of Pilgrim Congregational Church, UCC, Anacortes, Washington.

We come in our diversity
to be made whole, complete;
to offer those who'd share with us
a welcome full, replete
with inquiry and even doubt,
yet joyful in the dream
that sacredness reveals itself
in oneness, without seam.

Above all creeds, we value most
the sacred voice revealed
within each life, each life to come,
within a whole earth healed.
We see in scripture truths revealed
beyond the word, the phrase.
In these, we seek their wisdom, truth
deserving of our praise.

In Jesus, we find teacher, Christ,
embodying God's love
through mercy, justice, words of hope:
a sacred treasure trove
which we can share with all who walk
no matter what their course.
We honor one another's truths
through love and not through force.

Unfolding creativity
connects all life on earth.
It falls to us to partner, while
acknowledging each life's worth.
We join in covenant with earth
to honor it with care,
respecting places, and each life
in all time: everywhere.

Hymn tune: *Ellacombe*

Misleading ourselves

How ready, how facile we are
in speaking about the ineffable.
We offer with such certainty
what we do not, cannot know.

Our words, our images deceive us
into believing all can be made understandable,
but fail to recognize
we have been misled.
By ourselves.

Can't you understand anything?

Oh, the onus we place on words
as we employ them to capture,
convey essences, feelings, images
which are beyond all verbal snares.
But we ignore these difficulties
positing words, not alone as symbols,
but as possessing physical substance.

Our social intercourse relies upon words
carrying meanings we believe are shared
by others. We focus upon denotation
while disregarding connotation in our
use of words. We cast words as ingots of steel
rather than offering them as pliant lumps of clay.

Perhaps words should carry warning labels:
CAUTION: CONTENTS UNDER PRESSURE.
DO NOT USE IN ENCLOSED SPACES.
NOT APPROVED FOR EVERY USE
TO WHICH A SPEAKER OR WRITER
MAY WISH TO PUT IT. DO NOT TRY
TO USE SUCH WORDS AT HOME.

The folly in such a suggestion is obvious
as we consider employing words
to convey cautions regarding words.

Has the acquisition of language
been overrated?

Fall gown

Oh, let my autumn gown glow in
brilliant red and flaming gold.
May it dance with fall winds
until the music ends,
then drop in variegated folds
at my feet as I stand naked,
to shiver through another cold winter.

Perhaps there is something
to the stately, albeit unimaginative,
attire of nearby firs and cedars.
They are not objects of adoration
of the sort I have received.

But neither do they stand
for all the world to see
every knot and blemish
naked age has wrought.

Wisdom's candle

The flickering light of the
candle of wisdom
is dimmed in the inferno set ablaze
by the torch of my ignorance.

How memory works 101

There are times
when I try to imagine my brain
at work inside my skull.
Amid, across each concave sulcus ,
along each convex gyrus
impulses, part chemical, part electrical,
dart toward synapses
that don't really connect anything.
Once there, impulses
sail the gap aboard protein vessels,
signaling to the next neuron to fire-
   or not.

It is easier if I think of my memory
as a message board on which are
        taped
        stapled
        tacked
              notes
              scrawled reminders
              mementos
a few to remain long past their timeliness,
others to lose their grip and slip
prematurely into oblivion
defying all attempts to retrieve their contents.

At this stage in life, it is the slippage
to which I best relate.
Perhaps the synapses are growing wider,
harder to cross.
Or is it that there is a shortage of craft

to transport signals?
Maybe my circuitry has corroded through
misuse, lack of use, age itself.

I would end this treatise on a sapient note
but will not, for
I have forgotten what it was I set out to say.

Images of ending

If I have any say about the manner of my death,
I would like it to be a sharp period
struck hard at the end of a well-turned sentence.
No parentheses containing further explanation
or ellipsis implying there is more to come.

Most of all, I do not want to end
as a smudged, quavering line
left by a dull pencil meandering down the page
as if the holder fell asleep during a boring lecture.

Mother's Day Hymn, May 9, 2010

What images must we amend,
what ancient views set free
if we're to let the sacred learn
to be what she would be.

We fetter God in countless ways
in image and through word,
creating idols formed from clay.
A fettered God? Absurd.

We draw our God in human ways,
for that is all we know,
amazed when others stretch our gaze
and cause our God to grow.

Oh mother, father, sacred one
whose nurture does not wane;
in you have all things e'er begun;
in you will all remain.

'Twas sacred loins gave cosmos birth,
that sculpted Gaia's face.
From that same sacred all draw worth
that they might dwell in grace.

Mystery

We balk at the prospect of mystery,
preferring to act as if we should know,
could know, will know everything.

For many, knowing is just a matter of time:
time and appropriate technology.

Machines gigantic and minuscule
reveal the workings of the cosmos, ourselves.
We know so much: but not everything.

We seem to regard every mystery as requiring solution.
Rainbows, once symbols of promise and faithfulness
are, we now know, light refracted
through the prism of earth's atmosphere.
Does knowing this alter meanings
we attach to rainbows?

A flower's unfolding petals can be described
by a mathematical algorithm. Does this diminish
the joy we experience in fresh blossoms.

Oh, what we know, will yet know
and how we blench at the prospect that,
beyond all knowing, mystery will remain
like a beckoning lover desiring
to be appreciated for herself
without ever being understood
completely.

On a rainy afternoon

From the window by our kitchen table,
I watch birds in their variety assemble
on the feeders and in the nearby bushes.
Trees look greener following
many hours of cleansing rain.

I watch these in the belief
that we are, at base, of one substance,
one essence.
We share in life,
we all will know death.
There is comfort
in not feeling alone while I have these
as companions.

Let me hear you

Have I taken time today to hear you?
Listen to your story,
The song you sang this day.

If there is yet time, I pray that
My ears and heart will open,
For you have much to teach me
That I need to learn.

Prayer words

Prayer words:
therein resides the dilemma,
for our words are at least once-removed
from the formless source
on which prayer draws.

Perhaps prayer boils down to listening
more than thinking, or talking.
I sense that, when I begin talking,
either to myself or aloud to others,
prayer ends.

Prayers are communions:
times when we sit silently with sacredness,
draw common breath,
sense a closeness beyond comprehension,
know a peace that does indeed
surpass our understanding.
It is a moment that needs nothing
beyond the unspoken affirmation,
"Yes."

Remembrance

It's not like a ghost, really,
this sense of another's presence
after their death.

It is that they were so much a part
of familiar spaces,
occupying favorite chairs,
moving in a characteristic manner
from place to place,
tossing an over-the-shoulder comment
as they left the room.

At times, one can feel the need
to step aside to avoid
being in their way, or choose
another chair than theirs
so they will have a place to sit
when they re-enter the room,
as surely they will. As surely
they must.
They remain. Not tangibly,
but as a loving presence.

Sanctuary

Where shall we find sanctuary
in a world that affords
fewer and fewer places of shelter:
asylum for life of any kind?

Even refuge we might take in our own hearts
is subject to invasion by incessant demands
from beyond ourselves.
From those we make upon ourselves.

We construct presumed places of safety
fortified with thick, high walls of steel and stone,
place bars upon windows,
dig moats on all sides
in the belief these will render us invulnerable
to those who would attack.

Once inside, we cower in armored rooms
surrounded by guards and systems of surveillance.
To no avail, for we take into such places
the very selves from which we would escape.

If we are to find sanctuary,
it begins in this moment,
in ourselves.
If we are to know sanctuary,
   we will need to provide it.

The search for God

When I awoke this morning,
I spent several minutes
trying to recall where I put God
when I went to bed last night.

I remember talking to God for a few minutes
before going to sleep, as I do each night.
But this morning…
   where is God this morning?

Joyce is given to asking on such occasions,
"Where did you last have it?"
I know where was. At least I think I do.

Where on earth, or anywhere else,
did I put God, for goodness sake?
Now, I'll worry about this all day.

Should I pray to see if I hear God ringing?

Seeker's lament

How incomplete I am
for trying to know sacred spirit
through reliance on words
and the thoughts or images
they evoke.

My senses are attuned to survive in this world,
though they fall short of detecting
that which is not of this world:
that which is forever undetectable.

I believe holiness to be ineffable,
yet proceed to think, write,
talk glibly about God,
   whatever God is or isn't,
in the parlance of earthly existence.

Sacred,
unknowable beyond my knowing,
inaccessible beyond my strivings,
indescribable beyond my descriptions,
what on earth am I to do with you?

To sleep, perchance to dream?

During my nighttime intervals of sleep,
great thoughts,
even brilliant thoughts,
erupt from my unconscious,
though perhaps eruct is the better term,
sometimes full blown,
more often in bits and pieces.

Ideas emerge with an urgency to
"Write us down before we slip away."
But I know such insights
will remain with me until I wake.

Occasionally, they remain;
more frequently, they slide back into the abyss
of unconsciousness
as I continue to navigate the gossamer boundary
between sleep and wakefulness.

The thoughts that emerge often are fraught
with conflict, insoluble dilemmas which I,
like a knight errant,
am compelled to adopt as my quest,
to fulfill before I waken.

Then, there are those images that arrive
ringed in black: dark, depressive pronouncements
that drag me into a still deeper oblivion.

Who is it that takes over my brain while I sleep
to think on these things,
to continue to tear at the threads
of my already-raveled sleeve of care?

Sowing poems

Poems are creations of the moment:
   of a moment, really.
Seeds sown in random ideas and images
eventually reach a time to blossom.

What emerges from a time of writing
always is a surprise to me,
for it usually is a hybrid,
an unexpected interweaving of ideas
   that preceded it.

In a way, it is rather like emptying
a packet labeled "mixed flowers"
onto freshly-turned soil.

Tears to come

I have been skirting the verge of tears,
not out of avoidance, but having yet
to step fully into their presence.

Quite unexpectedly and publicly, they come,
bringing release.

Squeezing life

How do I squeeze the last drop from my life
without prolonging my days needlessly
and at great cost to those about me?

Is squeeze the right verb for what I want to do?

Rather than portray my life as a lemon
from which the last drop of juice needs to be pressed,
or a tube of toothpaste in its flattened death throes,

I prefer to regard life as a well
from which to dip and drink carefully, even then
leaving plenty for those who follow.

Thank you for listening

The week before last,
when I was young,
I used to experience a pang of guilt
when I turned off the radio mid-program,
for surely those speaking would know
I was no longer present to pay attention
to their efforts.

They knew,
and did not forgive me,
for the next time I switched on the radio,
they had moved on to something else.

Thanksgiving 2009

Give thanks in this season
for blessings past reason.
Give thanks for our larders stocked from the rich earth.
Remember those wanting
whose hunger is daunting.
Whose lot is from circumstance not lesser worth.

We cannot claim favor
that we blessings savor
as millions are starving despite all they do
to share with their neighbors
the fruit of their labors.
Oh that we might share in their charity, too.

Give thanks for each creature
whose life gift is featured
surrounded by dishes to round out the fare.
As life feeds the living,
we pause in thanksgiving,
remembering all those whose tables stand bare.

Hymn tune: *Let all things now living*

Lamentation

They bend to speak softly,
to listen to their dad living out his last days.
It is a conversation of privacy,
daughters to their beloved father.
They know what the days ahead hold.
Now is a time for loving smiles,
quiet laughter, gentle teasing,
brushing back thinning hair.

Compassionate sorrow.
Sorrowful compassion.

Let death arrive engulfed by love.
Let this last journey begin
swaddled in affection.
There is nothing better to do now
than to love in warm words,
gentle touches, soft kisses.

This will not end well:
only in release from a fading life.

Unending seeking

I labor to know what I will not,
cannot know.
In this, I am fellow traveler
with all who have ever,
will ever,
live.

What is this marvel we seek,
this nothingness, for surely it is not entity,
that has never been.

I will end
as I began
swirling in eternal unknowing.

Vanishing memory

The excavations grow larger,
like grains of sand tumbling
from the sides of holes dug on the beach.

I do not see the gaps growing,
but fall into them
as what once was
vanishes.

Waking

It is when I waken
that I am aware of having been asleep.

Dreams should have been a clue,
but they do not always come.

And what of that time
when I do not waken:
what then?
Will all this have been a dream?

Wind is forecast

Puffing at my window,
whistling round the sash,
wind gusts raise a ruckus
on their noisy dash.

Strong winds were predicted,
TV told us so.
Maps revealed directions
from which they would blow

and how strongly buffet
all within their way.
I think that I'll just cuddle
with a book today.

We do not kill

Oh the paths along which we guide those
who kill on our behalf.
Of course, we are not killers ourselves.
We hire those assigned to kill.
And it isn't exactly that we hire them to kill.
It's that what we order them to do requires killing.

It is of no matter that they might prefer not to kill:
would not have killed another human being,
or perhaps anything else,
had we not thrust the requirement upon them.

It is not on our heads
that circumstances in which we put them
are filled with bursts of light and explosion,
chatter of automatic weapons,
comrades who groan and fall about them.
These happen in war.
Anyone would kill to save self and comrades,
nation we say.
Anyone?

But *we* do not kill:
do not dispatch another human to death.
Nasty business, war.
Nasty, this war business.
It's just a bloody shame anyone needs to get hurt.

Whittlin' 2009-2010

From
And did I tell you
2009-2011

By what light do we guide our steps

Advent Hymn

By what light do we guide our steps,
by what beam set our course?
Is it by ancient legends' claims
or by old creed's stern force?
Is it not hope, is it not love
illumines how we wend?
Is it not toward justice for all
that we our labors bend?

Let us, then, walk toward sacredness
to fathom what faith holds
beyond grand symbols of times past,
from stories told of old.
May we find symbols for this day
to teach new hearts and minds,
directing us on pathways fresh
not knowing what we'll find.

The life set on a sacred way
is life shared with all things.
It is a hymn of wondrous joy
with which creation sings.
Is it not hope, is it not love
illumines how we live?
Is it not toward the worth of all
that we our struggle give?

Hymn tune: *Kingsfold*

Sing of promise, sing of coming

Advent Hymn

Sing of promise, sing of coming,
sing of light illumining
people of all faith and nations,
differing paths examining
what it means to seek the sacred
swaddled deep in mystery:
what it means to walk in wonder
writing earth's new history.

Sing in awe of cosmos swirling,
spreading as it spirals on
without limit or direction,
always birthing: never done.
Infinite in all dimensions,
born of first star's birthing burst.
We are moved to probe the mysteries
urged on by our wonder's thirst.

Sing the stories of our history
handed down from age to age,
told by those of all persuasion,
prophesied by seer and sage.
These are meant to paint a picture
which our feeble wit can hold.
All is meant to sing of oneness
which all living things enfolds.

Hymn tune: *Hymn to joy*

Let each new day an advent be

Let each new day an advent be,
each hour a freshened store
of all life's spirit offers up
to what her lushness bore.

May every breath of advent sing
in voice imbued with awe
as we greet moments in their line
replete with gifts galore.

For advent tells of what can be,
of what is yet to come.
Its gaze is on that yet ahead:
a future yet to plumb.

The advent images we hold
are from old stories shaped
into poor shepherds, eastern seers
who moved in richness draped.

Let advent bring new songs of hope
to ravaged, weary earth
as we anticipate anew
what comes as a new birth.

Hymn tune: *St. Anne*

In each of life's newborn moments

Advent hymn

In each of life's newborn moments
may we a fresh advent know
as we carol out a message
which from eager heart o'erflows.
Ours is not to cast eyes backward
toward a time and place of yore
but to turn heart and attention
to what life still holds in store.

Whether led to cross wide desert
or to watch from mountain's height,
ours it is to journey onward
through the day and through the night.
In the city or the village,
wherever our lives may lead,
ours it is to birth each moment
as a gift from sacred seed.

We are not to cling to moments
as fruition of our days
but to move through each in wonder,
leading us along our ways.
Moments pregnant with new being
calling us to live renewed.
Moments, lives in rich succession
with a sacredness imbued.

Hymn tune: *Hymn to joy*

"Let the words of my mouth…"

This is a day when I search for soft words
with which to speak, think, write.

Gentle words befitting a late summer afternoon
in which the only distraction
is the whirr of a power mower in a nearby yard.

This is a moment when I feel smoothed,
    without sharp edges,
a stone shaped by water and grit grinding,
smoothing it for a thousand generations.

My ideas turn slowly,
without the haste they often display
pressing for expression.

It is a day when I feel at peace,
unwilling to dredge for thoughts
that harbor potential for evoking rancor.

In these days of strident, hateful utterances,
now seems a time that requires thoughtful,
careful words
offered rather than hurled,
accepting rather than rejecting,
affirming rather than demeaning.

May mine be among them.

And did I tell you…?

A gathering of friends of long-standing
destined at some point in the conversation
to look backward in memory,
forward in prospect.

Inquiries arise about one another's health,
usually to be dealt with in a kind of shorthand
so conversation can return
to the brighter agenda of the day.

Laughter always seems to be an ingredient on such
occasions stemming from what was,
what is,
what we hope will be.

Other friends, living and not,
find their way into the exchange.
Connections lasting many decades
are recalled, updated, celebrated.

The sweetness of such events mixes with the bitter
as we acknowledge,
usually individually and tacitly,
that we may never again be together like this.

Is it this realization that helps people perfect
the fine art of lingering?

And the greatest of these…

It seems that very little changes in life.
People dominate other people.
People resist domination by others and,
usually, suffer in the ensuing conflict.

We are told, "…these abide:
faith, hope, and love." We are also told,
"The greatest of these is love." Really?
Where? In whom?

It is as though love always seems
to end up being suppressed by enmity
between individuals, tribes, nations.
It is as if love is itself enemy
of some more basic human motive.

If this is true, I cannot change it.
The only change I can make
is to let love abide in me,
guide me in my actions toward others,
toward the earth, myself.

Annual pruning

Each year in January
a gardener with crew in tow
arrives to prune our apple trees
and tend to overgrowth
in other shrubs and trees in our yard.

We could leave the job to the local deer herd,
but they prune only those shrubs
they find edible and end their tree pruning
four to five feet from the ground.
The final product is, generously put, odd.

A growing aversion to ladders,
stiff hands and backs,
along with a desire to stay out of the cold,
deter us from a task that has been ours
until recent years. Oh, and knowing
how to do it properly. That too.

Joyce cuts back the daffodils and tulips
and, with a modicum of help from me,
tackles the roses each year.

Together we prune remains
of a lovely clematis that winds its way up
an ornate trellis designed and built
by our son-in-law, Ray, shortly after
we moved here in 2001.
We'll dig into the Mambresia soon.
The major pruning gets done
by others these days.

I have undergone pruning over the years
so that activities I once claimed as my own
get passed on to family
or those we pay to do them.

I continue to try to bear fruit with my life,
but it may be less abundant
than I like to think it once was.
Life does its own pruning year-to-year,
trimming back farther and farther
to find still-vital wood.

Birds of a feather

Pigeons huddle in a tight row
along the power line
leaving scant space bird from bird.

Do they permit "cuts" in line,
as school children are wont to take,
requiring the whole gathering
to loosen its collective grip on the wire
so it can shuffle
one way or the other?

Is that grumbling I hear?
A warning to avoid walking
under the congregation at that moment
lest at least one disgruntled member responds
in a passive-aggressive manner?

As old as the wind

The flapper in the vent
above our kitchen range
taps out a one-note tattoo
signaling arrival of predicted winds.
Outside, stirring of nearby trees
confirms its report.

Later, I will venture out
to feel wind's push:
move against its mischievous gusts
that try to catch me off guard and
pitch me off my feet.

We don't, so far so I know,
use the expression,
"As old as the wind,"
though I think it an apt one
as we locate ourselves as newcomers
among currents
that have moved as they will,
where they will
   forever.

Autumn reflection

The deck umbrella flaps,
drying itself in the first winds of autumn
before I store it under the house.

Summer ended, fall followed amid rainstorms,
reminding us of its seasonal trademark.

It now is time to carry small umbrellas,
wear jackets that close tightly around us, and
fasten around the neck to repel wind and driving rain.
It is the season for sturdy shoes,
lighter footwear pushed to the back of the closet
until spring.

Fall is a season of alchemy
when nature again works the long sought-after wonder
of turning elements to gold.

Leaves lose their grasp on stems
spinning lightly downward
to spread a gilded cloak over the earth.

It is to the collection of these golden offerings
Joyce and I turn time and attention
as we prepare the lawn and garden for the winter
that comes to everything.

Bay waters

Our path to the gazebo above Sunset Bay
passes along a bluff. Below,
there is always the reverberation of water
rolling onto the shore,
sometimes in loud washes,
most often lapping gently.

The water and its sound are there
as they have been for eons:
as they will be for eons to come.

There is something reassuring
about knowing some things
are ancient in their histories,
long-lasting into their futures.

Quite unlike me and my kind.

Busted

Recently, the poetry police
busted (as in apprehended) me
for wantonly tagging
(as in spray painting graffiti on)
the hallowed halls of American literature.

I had no defense. Caught mid-rhyme
and with a dangling modifier to boot,
they had me cold (as in no way to weasel out).
As punishment, they fired my muse,
and suspended indefinitely my poetic license.
Looking up my record, they questioned
whether my license was ever issued legally:
indeed, was ever issued at all.
I pleaded ignorance;
they countered, "No contest."
At least the embarrassment and expense of a trial
will be avoided.

There may be a snag in this for you.
Someone casually mentioned that
a charge of aiding and abetting
might be brought against those
who have encouraged my efforts over the years.

You may be hearing from the Poet Laureate.

Choices

What fate awaits a species
that grooms its clutch for war:
that prides itself on conquest
in endless press for more?
Will humankind be ever
torn in identity:
one nature deep compassion,
the other enmity?

What fate awaits a species
for which the good looms large
but chooses to turn blessing
into lethal barrage?
We search to learn life's mysteries
so life can richer be,
yet sacrifice our genius
to hateful enmity.

Pray one might come to teach us
to love as we are loved:
to live among each other
our vengeful bent removed.
Would we believe such teaching:
live out its loving theme?
Or would we slay the teacher,
renouncing peace as dream?

  Hymn tune: *Aurelia*

Casting the first stone

Today, on this 4th day of January, ,
I began a project despite the imminence
of my 74th birthday.

Henceforth, when Joyce and I walk to Burrow's Bay,
I intend to pick up a stone from the beach
and fling it into the water,
in time yielding a causeway
from the shore where we stand
to Burrow's Island a half mile distant.

The Coast Guard or some boating coalition
doubtless will complain about my project,
but sometimes,
a guy just has to follow his dream.

Christmas confession

My name is Densley. I am a package shaker.

Even as a child, I crawled stealthily
beneath our Christmas trees
searching for labels bearing my name.
Finding them, out they came so I could gently,
shake each one in an attempt to identify contents.

I could recognize pajamas or shirts
by the softness of their packages.
No need to shake those. After a gentle
and, I hoped, undetectable investigation,
it was important to put each package
into its original position, leaving no evidence at all
of my trespass.

Yes, I was a closeted shaker.

I aimed for the square and cubed packages:
ones that might hold…my imagination ran wild
as I tried to recall hints I had been dropping
since Halloween: of list of wants
enumerated while seated on Santa's knee
in the tenth floor Toyland of Meier and Frank.

Grown older, I still shake gifts of Christmas
to see what they might hold.
Unlike my explorations of childhood,
I try to keep an open mind
on what Christmas holds each year,
for the essence of the season
has become for me one of mystery.

Mystery beyond all imagining:
mystery surpassing all understanding.

And did I tell you 2009-2011

Come and get it

We grow restive about the place
we claim as ours at life's great table
even though it is to the host this decision falls.

Sometimes, we spar like birds at a feeder
as we fend off those we deem ill-suited
for the host's company, our company,
even the food we claim to be our own.

We cannot comprehend the possibility
of there being more than enough
for all to eat.

It is not our place to send any away,
but to invite all who hunger to sit,
even offering to stand so there will be room.

Closeness

I enjoy being close to people.
Not to every one.
But to the people with whom
I share special moments.

Closeness conjures up
so many images.
At the moment, a virus

has taken residence
in my body.
I do not regard this as being "close,"
so much as an invasion.

Being close to another creature,
whether human or not
has a cherishing quality to it.
It is this sense of cherishing
that yields a feeling of intimacy.

I am fortunate in enjoying
a sense of intimacy with family and
many friends who serve
as emotional benchmarks for my life.

Whether I serve in this way for them,
is not mine to say.
That someone would see me in this way
is humbling.

The only time I explicitly asked someone
to be close to me was over 51 years ago,
when I invited Joyce to become my wife.

Since then, being close has been more of
an open and voluntary invitation.

No agent will call.

Color crayons

Remember those late summer excursions
to the five and dime just before school took up
right after Labor Day?
It was the occasion to buy school supplies:
pencils, a Pink Pearl eraser, a thick, red-covered
Jumbo tablet and a new box of crayons.

If the budget allowed,
you might even get to take home a pencil box
in which to store your newly-purchased treasures.
One of the hard choices for me on such expeditions
was buying crayons.

Early on, a thin box of ten or twelve basic colors
was sufficient for my task as well as for my talent.
Then, the Crayola Company began producing
bigger and bigger collections of color crayons
including shades like peach and flesh.
Red, blue, green, purple, black and white
would no longer suffice.

The standard, if family income permitted,
became a four-tiered regiment of
neatly-pointed ranks of colors that would
rival the palette, perhaps prick the envy,
of many an established artist.

Fortunately, there was a medium sized box.
Working with this box required an inexact blending of
colors to achieve more exotic hues. Clearly,
this was a Plymouth alongside the Cadillac
parked in the desks of other kids.

We never bought crayons for Sunday School classes.
What we used there came from an old hard-sided box,
perhaps even an old cigar box that no one would
admit to having smoked its contents.
The crayons clearly were veterans of decades
of misuse by children
who obviously knew nothing
about taking care of such treasures.

These fragments, for none was a complete crayon,
usually were about half the size or less of a new crayon,
often with only part, maybe even none, of its original
paper tube, and were almost always blunt from little
kids pressing too hard on them.
It wasn't surprising to find a blue, green, or red crayon
with one flat side, used, in all likelihood,
to fill in a field of grass, the sky, or side of a barn.

Although the Sunday School crayons were a motley
collection resembling those who used them,
they were serviceable unless the user
felt the need to draw a sharp line to enclose
or color close to the edge.

Somehow, associating with the cast offs
and avoiding drawing lines too distinctly
seemed like a good message
to offer Sunday School kids in those days.

Consolation

In my rare, slap-it-together attempts at carpentry,
pieces don't always fit the way the way I intend.

Such occasions call for a small something
to fill a gap, stop a wobble, or just hold pieces in place
while I take care of something else.

I have been known to carve small wooden wedges,
fold paper several times, or do whatever I needed
to compensate for my lack of precision.
I always have felt a pang of guilt over this.

So, what do I find these days in lumber stores
but cellophane packets of ready-made shims.

Though not advertised as such,
these are first-aid kits for occasions
when pieces don't fit the way they should
leaving a gap,
creating a wobble,
falling apart when the builder
turns attention to something else.

My discovery provides new insight
to the Biblical passage,
"All have shimmed and fallen short..."

And did I tell you 2009-2011

Do I really *need* this?

An ad in today's mail: "Isn't it time you had
the beautiful bathroom you deserve?"

Other than on occasions of need,
I don't think much about bathrooms,
even our own.
If a bathroom is close at hand, clean,
has an air quality that sustains life,
is properly plumbed,
I am satisfied.

But do I deserve even this much.
Do I deserve a bathroom at all?
Is there a right, divine or otherwise,
to a bathroom of any kind?
Let alone a "beautiful bathroom"?

I'm glad when places I visit
have bathrooms close at hand.

Most people of the world are not so fortunate,
making their environments
unhealthful, malodorous, messy.

Do they have as much right to a bathroom
as I do? I expect so.
But does any of us deserve
a beautiful bathroom?

When it comes down to it, what about
just assuring toileting facilities,

sewage treatment for the people of the world
before we pamper ourselves
with unnecessary beauty in a room
where we shouldn't spend so much time anyway?

Earth hymn

Earth resounds with anthems
hymned by all her children
in harmonies, dissonances,
rhythms, melodies:
in awe-inspiring wonder.

May we tune our senses
to hear and join these anthems
as we remain aware how
what we sing blends
with lines sung by others.

None of us sings alone.

Eighty-eight names

Eighty eight names now appear on the memorial
at Joint Base Lewis-McCord near Tacoma.
They are names of combatants killed in our wars
in Iraq and Afghanistan, though some died
closer to home while still in training.

Most are young names,
hardly out of the package in which they came.
But isn't this as it has always been in war:
old men don't go to war. They send children:
usually other people's children
who are deemed more malleable, trainable.
They would deny expendable.

Did these, their names carved in stone,
aspire to this as their legacy? Or,
did they have other, goals:
marriage, children, career?
A long life?

Do those who erect
and fill such memorials with names
ever do so with a sense of guilt? Regret?
Is a name's inscription an admission of failure
by a nation which holds out the promise to its young
that they can be whatever they wish to be?

Encountering sacredness

I've never slept Jacob-like
with a stone for my pillow.
Perhaps this is but one of many reasons
God has never selected me to dream of angels
ascending and descending a celestial stairway.

My experiences with holiness
have always been more pedestrian,
arriving without blaring trumpet,
glaring light,
a heavenly host singing divinely.

Sacredness has, I think,
always addressed me in subtle ways,
often when I am alone, and
usually in lower-case letters.

I have had no Damascus Road experience.
My awakenings to sacred presence
have been more glacial in nature,
grinding ponderously, imperceptibly
across the scarred landscape of my life.

Yet, I expect sacredness is present even today.
In what, in whom, will I discover it?

End of year musing

There is a richness
in the image of an hour glass draining
its grains of sand from top to bottom.
It conveys a sense
of nothing having been lost.
Inverting the glass uses the same sand
to begin measuring again.

There is none of this in what
a calendar provides
where we tear off or turn to a new page.
What we have lived is unceremoniously wadded,
tossed, recycled.
Reminders of sometimes important events
scribbled in the margins are lost.

Perhaps the symbolic glass
we should lift at year's end
is the bulb of the hour glass with the toast,
"See you again."

Join the dance into a future

Join the dance into a future
filled with holiness and light,
leaving evermore behind us
doleful dirges of the night.
Let us celebrate a new day
praising sacred manifest.
God is in us, with us ever,
dwelling as our sacred guest.

Raise our hands with all things living
in a circling dance of life,
clapping, turning to the music
of an earth set free from strife.
Strike the tambour, cue the pipers,
shake the tambourines in joy,
for to us has come God's wisdom
through a homeless baby boy.

No one nation holds all wisdom,
no one people lift the light.
It will take all life together
to escape the grip of night.
Trim our lamps, push back the darkness,
hold them high to show the way
toward the source of holy wisdom:
toward God's new and brighter day.

Hymn tune: *Holy manna*

Evolution at work

Midway through a morning hike around
Shannon Point,
we paused at the Marine Center
to talk with a young woman about her research
into the dietary habits of crab larvae.

Crab larvae are what she called
"opportunistic eaters,"
devouring whatever they find.

As I listened, I thought,
"That sounds a lot like me."

She went on to say their eating pattern
is not always beneficial for them.

That sounded a lot like me, too,
and I wondered, "How did my kind
ever make it this far?"

Exile

Where are our sites of exile?
Our Babylonia, Elba, Siberia?
Our "far countries"?

Where are those places where we are to…
 but what is it we are to do in exile?
Not do in exile?
Who are we to be, not be
 in exile?

Is it the disconnect from identity
exile brings
that inflicts its harshest
 punishment?

We are creatures of identity,
 place, relationships.
When these disappear,
personhood vanishes.

To whom will it fall to beckon us,
 "Come home"?

For whom shall we strong voices raise

For whom shall we strong voices raise
as hordes in silence cower
oppressed for who they are and think
by those who wield harsh power.

So many quail in silent fear
as they oppression flee.
It falls to all to lift a song
whose message sets them free.

We do not sing for selves alone
but for an earth entire.
To hold our song, not sing at all,
is to with power conspire.

Hymn tune: *St. Anne*

And did I tell you 2009-2011

Getting in the word last

Finding the right word,
sometimes, finding any word at all,
can be next to impossible.

Words hold potential
to be offerings of loving beauty,
but they also can degenerate
into mawkish utterances
grown of awkwardness.

Words, as we learn in times of pain,
do not, cannot carry
the depth and richness of feeling
conveyed in silent companionship,
a held hand,
an understanding smile,
a gentle, warm embrace.

We should treat occasions
when we do not find words
as gifts that permit us to let
our actions carry the messages
of our compassion.

Good company

It used to be that
whenever snow cloaked the ground
"cool and crisp and even,"
I looked forward to walks
across fields where there were no footprints,
where no one had broken through
the crust of smooth, glistening whiteness,
where I could hear my boots scrunch
as they reached for traction beneath
the snow's brittle face.

Anymore, I seldom walk
through unbroken snow
and avoid walking through snow altogether
lest the scrunch I hear
is of an old hip or elbow striking
ice-glazed pavement skulking about
in wait for the unaware, unsteady, unwise.

Our house is warm from the combination
of a winter sun shining
through the south-facing deck window
and the labors of a gas furnace in the garage.
I no longer have anything to prove
about my mobility
so elect to remain indoors.

There is no reason
to surround my feet with more than soft slippers
that scuff as I walk to the kitchen
to brew another cup of coffee,

then sit sipping it while still hot
with an old man's leisure
as I look out on another white day.

As I recall, Good King Wenceslas
looked out on snow cool, crisp, and even
that lay round about.

I always enjoy thinking myself in good company.

Summer reflection

There are mornings when I enter the garden
only to find no fruit to pick;

just a few bird-pecked remains
dangle from the limbs.

I remove the sampled remnants, leaving
a few leaves to allow sunlight to reach the vines

hoping this hastens a ripening
of what remains.

How shall we behold the wonder?

Epiphany

How shall we behold the wonder
of a sacred manifest
in all things, both seen and unseen:
praying we will be its guest.
Through our knowledge, we seek wisdom,
but true wisdom's not gained thus.
We set out to capture wisdom,
but it's wisdom captures us.

Light beyond all brilliance gleaming,
bringing sight to ready eyes.
Immanence surpassing knowing:
beyond knowledge, ever wise.
Through our knowledge, we seek wisdom,
but true wisdom's not gained thus.
We set out to capture wisdom,
but it's wisdom captures us.

What we see and know is portion
of enlightenment still bound
by delimiting perception:
never through pure reason found.
Through our knowledge, we seek wisdom,
but true wisdom's not gained thus.
We set out to capture wisdom,
but it's wisdom captures us.

From dark night of superstition,
we pursue a holy light
shed upon all lands and people:
honoring all life's birthright.
Through our knowledge, we seek wisdom,
but true wisdom's not gained thus.
We set out to capture wisdom,
but it's wisdom captures us.

Hymn tune: *Beecher*

I'll be back with you in one moment

Where do familiar names and words go
when I try to retrieve them mid-conversation?
Do they crouch behind one another,
don disguises to avoid recognition?

It's not that these names and words are lost forever
but that they are lost at all sparks annoyance.
That they are lost mid-sentence
introduces the specter of senescence
marked by an early, perhaps not-so-early, dementia.

Is this why synonyms were invented?
They may not be as precise in meaning as the original
but usually get me by in a pinch.
It is at that point the prodigal word
saunters in smiling innocently
wondering what the fuss is about.

And did I tell you 2009-2011

That awkward stage--again

*Awkward (adjective): clumsy or ungainly. As in,
"He's an awkward old duffer."*

The older I get, the more I regress
to earlier stages of awkwardness.
Perhaps, it's not regression at all.
Maybe I only imagined
becoming nimble as I ripened.

I make no claim about having been a model of grace
when younger — as in yesterday.
For one thing, I never fully trusted my body
to carry out my instructions.
Perhaps my instructions were themselves
awkward and undecipherable.

Long ago, I learned not to wear
light-colored pants and shirts
for spills and smudges promptly betrayed
my awkwardness at feeding myself.

While I momentarily entertain the idea
of going about without clothing,
or only the minimum required by public decree,
I remember the last time I spilled hot coffee on myself.
Perhaps a body-shielding, lead-lined loin cloth
would compensate for my lack of grace.

This is how things are for me at 74.
I accept Joyce's arm or that of one of our children
when they detect a misstep in my gait.

Activities requiring anything
beyond the most rudimentary agility
I leave to others.

Texting and cell phone use while walking
should be primary offenses at age 74
subject to being cited by the ambulation police.
Perhaps my present awkwardness
is life's way of imposing a temporal symmetry,
although I recoil at the prospect
of one day again moving about on all fours.

In a word

Creatures of words,
our vocabularies can be woefully inadequate
for tasks to which we attempt to put them.
Paraphrasing the Apostle Paul,
"The words I would say, I do not say.
Those I say, would that I had not said them."

For me, finding the right word
can be akin to sorting through the small,
multi-drawer cases
standing at the end of my work bench.
Each drawer holds
its own miscellany of antiquated contents
I have retained well beyond their usefulness.

When I need a bolt or nut of a given size and shape,
I usually dash immediately
to the professionally-kept, properly labeled cases
of a local hardware store
instead of rummaging fruitlessly through my own collection.
So it often is with my words.

But, like a household emergency
that precludes dashing to town for just the right part,
I have to turn for correct word
in what is at hand: apt or not.
Words I disinter from my verbal memory
may be rust-covered, totally unsuitable
for the task to which I would put them:
some no longer being suitable for any task.

If anything argues for a special vocabulary drawer
it is the need for words that carry healing, comfort,
easing of another's burden.

Such words don't have to be new or fancy.
Old ones may do quite well:
"Can you forgive me?"
"I am sorry to have caused you pain."
"I grieve with you in your loss."
"Can we start over?"
"Thank you."
"Please."

Infernal, internal switchboard

The switchboard of my brain
can be as muddling in its efforts
to route messages from one place to another
as any commercial telephone service.

I swear what I hear on some attempts
at conversation with myself
are busy signals or intercepts like,
"That number is no longer in service," or
"To dial that number, you must first dial a 1-0 and the area code," or
"Recheck the number and dial again."

When informed the number no longer works,
I mutter something like,
"But I used this number just yesterday."
"That was yesterday," is the scornful reply.
"Perhaps whoever you were trying to reach
has moved, died, or just doesn't want to
respond to more of your incessant pestering."

There even seem to be times when,
just as I am ready to quit trying and hang up,
there is a "click" on the line,
as if someone has been listening in.
You don't suppose….

Did I ever tell you about the alien abduction
I experienced as a child?

Life's course

Consider the twists and turns of life
with its predilection
for reversing direction on a dime
before sending us
racing helter-skelter along
an altogether unanticipated path.

This is not something we see looking ahead,
only gazing back at where we've been:
at where we
think we've been.

"Who would have thought…?"
we say to no one in particular
as we try to sketch a line
from where we think we started
to where we calculate we are now.

On a map, the route a life takes
probably resembles less the bold,
direct highways drawn on maps.
and more the twisting, faint squiggles,
dotted streaks,
that meander through countryside,
along rivers, over mountain passes
passable only during certain seasons
and even then at great risk.

What if our life map contained nothing
beyond names of rivers, mountain ranges and peaks,
lakes, basins and glaciers

without superimposed lines
denoting roads, and trails:
none of the lines along which most people
move from place to place?
None of the lines intended to keep us from leaving
the beaten track.

In youth, usually at the urging of elders,
we strain for exquisite clarity in life goals
and how to go about achieving them
as directly, as quickly
as possible.

Guidance often resembled delivering
a road atlas showing how to move
from point A to point B
in the most expeditious manner.

Aging, we grow to understand
the route we take
to be as important,
sometimes more important,
than where we thought it
was supposed to lead.

We learn that the richest part of experience,
the most beautiful part of life
often came from leaving the trail and
striking off cross country
to discover what mysteries lay hidden
beyond the crest of the next hill.

And did I tell you 2009-2011

May others sing our message

*Dedicated to the memory of
Laurel Mae Loomis Malcomson*

We are not born to live our days
as if held by strong tether
but to stretch out to know the world:
to see life joined together.
All life sprang forth from single source
and toward one end it's headed.
Our ending is the price of life
to be embraced, not dreaded.

The limits we are prone to set
as bound'ries for our living
are starting points for knowing more
through open heart, and giving.
We parcel out our lives in shares
between ourselves and others,
neglecting all came forth as one
from common, sacred mother.

May we not live our lives tight-shut
but with arms thrown wide open,
as we embrace life's every gift
and learn from each its lesson.
We know the period we call life
and know that season's passage.
As season's done and life is gone,
may others sing our message.

Tune: *I cannot help but singing*

Mistake making

Please forgive me.
I've not been working
at this business of life very long
so I still make mistakes:
a great many mistakes.

It's been only 74 years since I began:
as a child, really.
If mistake-making prodigies had been recognized
back then, I would have been famous.
Perhaps they were.
Perhaps I was without knowing it.

There were lots of mistakes then.
Come to think of it,
there always have been lots of mistakes.

What I have found with advancing age
is that life is a combination
of repeating old mistakes
even as I discover brand new ones.
I repeat some mistakes
but never seem to learn from them
as I have been told I should.

But it's the new ones that really catch me up:
those I never see coming.
Those that snigger at me
as if to underscore my sense
of universal ineptness.

One thing I think I have learned,
though I offer no guarantee of this,
is that a mistake is not the same as a sin.
This took me a long time to understand.

Some mistakes are sins, I expect,
though I worry less about them than I used to.
Perhaps I should.
I may be mistaken.

Pulses of life

There are pulses to life:
pulses we ignore at our peril.

There are rhythms in the exquisite
working of our bodies:
inhaling, exhaling, the throbbing of our hearts,
the coursing of blood through our miles of vessels.

There are rhythms to waking and sleeping,
arousal and calm.

All nature pulses as life begins, ripens, ends
so new life might begin, ripen, end.

Life is not intended to last forever,
but to give way to what is yet to come
in whatever form newness favors.

Once broken

When they are broken,
some things never heal
despite splints, crutches,
therapy, braces.

Human spirit is like this
when trust,
hope
are sorely damaged,
leaving a heart
   forever damaged.

Tensile strength of spirit
cannot be quantified
to predict at what pressure it will break
or severity of damage when it does

but we see it,
hear it
over and over
by the limp that remains.

Orienteering

I would not have lasted long
on the exodus from Egypt
to some unknown land called "promised."

It's likely I would early on have
grumbled, whimpered,
"When will we be there?" or
urged Moses and Aaron to turn back:
return to the
"It's not great, but it's at least familiar"
districts of life.

I'm not a wilderness kind of guy:
not a survivor in adversity,
nor a live-off-the-land sort.
Wilderness may be an interesting
place to visit, but I would opt
for not staying long:
certainly not for forty years,
forty days or even far less.

Perhaps it comes from growing up
in southeast Portland in the 1950's.
There weren't many wildernesses there
save for a few lots covered in
Scotch Broom. Nor were there many
"dark nights of the soul" occasions
in my young life.

Sidewalks led to and from school and
pretty much anywhere else I wanted to go.

Street corners were marked by
names and numbers and
in what section of town they were located.

This isn't to say life didn't get ratty
at times: that I didn't feel lonely or
like a failure sometimes.
But, so far as I can recall,
I never felt totally alone:
wholly on my own to survive by
whatever few wits I could muster.

Still, there were the niggling
"Could I…"
"Would I…"
"Should I…"questions.
Would I know what to do?
Could I do it?
Should I do it?

It's disappointing to reach my advanced age
still harboring doubts about these things.

Our children die

Our children die.
Not of injury or disease of their own
but from harassment,
tortures, demonic willful acts of others.
They die from the sickness of hatred
toward any who are different.

Our children die.
Not other people's children:
our children, for all children
are ours to nurture,
protect, and love.

Our children die
because other children
have not grown enough
to celebrate differences
in our shared humanity.

Our children die,
will continue to die,
until the twin perversities
of fear and hatred
are dissolved in the crucible
of compassion.

So much for the old year

The old year displays no evidence of fatigue
as it tumbles over itself
in a rush toward midnight.

Does it move with such alacrity
because it knows
there is another year
waiting to receive the baton of time?

Does it expect to slip into the wash of history
clinging to a sense of satisfaction over its efforts?

And what of the new year?
Does it wait eagerly in the wings,

or does it cower while listening for its cue,
secretly hoping the show will close
before it has to step on stage

thereby removing any need for it
to make an appearance at all?

It seems worth pondering
as our clocks inch toward midnight.

Sweet water

Where is sweet water
so we might quench our aching thirst?

All about us stands water grown stale,
polluted,
the only source of refreshing
for most creatures of earth.

What have we done with sweet water
that burbled from earth's caverns,
tumbled in mountain stream to the sea?

What have we done to lakes,
to the sea, mother of all water?

Willful ignorance of how earth works
has led us to create deserts
through which we are destined to stumble
vainly scratching earth's crust for water,
bemoaning our fate,
fixing blame beyond ourselves for water's
absence.

We are the prodigal who claimed his portion
of a father's wealth only to squander it.
Alas, there will be no forgiving father
to welcome us home,
to quench our thirst,
for we have poisoned his wells,
squandered his legacy.

In desperation, we angrily strike our staff
against rocks demanding
they break open,
spill water once again.

But rocks remain closed,
silent,
gazing in wonder on our folly.

The well

The rusted pulley hangs from the well's roof,
squeals as the rope runs over it
dropping its dilapidated bucket into blackness.

I cannot count the times
bucket has made this descent
to rise again with fresh,
life-sustaining offerings.

My pail seems to fall farther now
and I think I hear it bump against
the well's bottom.

When I raise it to drink,
its water tastes brackish,
feels more gritty
than even just last week.

Perhaps I need a new bucket.

We are people of a journey

What is next along our journey?
What adventures wait in store
for a people stretching forward
to new provinces explore?
We are people of a journey,
travelers in sacred space.
Lay down all that would be burden:
all that would bind us in place.

Shall we in our Egypt linger
captives of abusive might,
or will we life's myst'ries hazard,
risking all in perilous flight?
We are people of a journey,
travelers in sacred space.
Lay down all that would be burden:
all that would bind us in place.

Will those promises we're offered
travel with us as we leave
all we've known for generations,
that we've fixed on to believe?
We are people of a journey,
travelers in sacred space.
Lay down all that would be burden:
all that would bind us in place.

Fording river, crossing desert,
weak from hunger, disbelief,
We seek not for place, but freedom,
searching ever, our motif.

We are people of a journey,
travelers in sacred space.
Lay down all that would be burden:
all that would bind us in place.

Hymn tune: *Beach spring*

Let us raise our hymns anew

We dwell within a unity,
in covenant with all
who bear the fruit of ancient seed
strewn o'er a fragile ball.

The elements which form all life
are spawn of fiery gust
that birthed a cosmos limitless:
into which earth was thrust.

We've storied this in metaphor
of how all came to be:
employed invention as our fact,
staunch credence as our key.

May we respond to doubt with hope,
probe mystery with awe.
Then let us raise our hymns anew
as we on wonder draw.

Hymn tune: *Ellacombe*

What we do for love

My anxiety level rose
when IT made its annual February appearance:
the tissue-paper-covered white cube
adorned with small, suggestive red hearts,
that sat at the front of the classroom.

Oh, it wasn't just the great unknowing
surrounding giving and receiving
store-bought valentines in small white envelopes
to and from classmates.

It was having to use our snub-nosed, injury-proof
steel scissors to create symmetric, oversized
red hearts for our mothers that more adept kids
(usually the girls) bordered with faux lace ribbon.

It wasn't that I didn't love my mother,
as much as a boy can love anything beyond himself
at that age except maybe a dog.

It wasn't that I didn't like to give my mother things,
as much as a boy can who didn't have an allowance
that stretched beyond a periodic penny-candy or two
at Andy's grocery.

It was that I, at seven or eight years of age,
had yet to learn how to cut out a
valentine that looked like something
other than a grossly misshapen cirrhotic liver.

Yes, fold the paper in two (if you want a
crease down the middle of your mother's heart),

draw half-a-heart with your smudgy, number two pencil
and try not to erase it with your even more smudged
eraser, and then....cut.

Cut slowly along the line
with those scissors designed,
as were all things during those tender years,
for right-handed children: even our desks,
neglecting sorely the needs of those of us who were
not righties.

It all unfolded, dare I say collapsed, like this:
Step 1: Fold the paper in two and draw the outline
of one-half of your heart.
Step 2: Cut slowly, following the line....drat.
Step 1: Fold the paper in...
Step 2: Cut slowly...nuts.
Step 1: and on and on until the teacher
banned me from the paper supply closet.

Perhaps it was at this time
I began to write verse.
Asymmetric, no-fold-down-the-middle verse
that didn't require use of right-handed
tools of torture and ridicule that squeaked out,
"Loser!" with every squeeze of the handle.

Many years later, it was one of my verses we sang
when we gathered for mom's memorial service
in 1989.

I still write and still don't cut out valentines.
Don't expect one.

Word woman

*To Thelma Palmer
Poet, teacher, friend*

Word woman.
Plucks up a word
holds it to the sun
sees how it bends the light
this way and that
as she turns it
in her hand.

Word woman.
Holds a word
to her ear
listens to its song
hears its whispered secrets
its raging lament
its paean of joy.

Word woman.
Presses a word
against her cheek
feels it responding
to her warmth.

Word woman.
Selects words
that look, hear,
feel just right
in her heart.

From
Legacy
2011-2012

A gradual healing

There is so much we do not,
will not ever, know,
much less understand.

This is not so much a reason
to avoid seeking knowledge
and understanding
as it is an acknowledgement of our
finiteness in the face
of the infinite.

It often is only with the passage of time
that we begin to see, understand
what is at first hidden from us:
see enough, understand enough
to begin releasing its hold
bit by
  bit by
    bit.

A richer walk

My tendency to philosophize about the end of life
gets its comeuppance
when death touches down close by.

My walk through life
has been filled with trail-marking people:
those who have served as sources of direction,
bringers of joy,
lenders of light to my path.

Many of these markers continue to guide me:
may that be the case so long as a portion of my trail
is yet to be walked with them.

Even in their absence,
many of those who originally
helped me set my course and remain on it,
exert their influence through memory.

The beauty of any path, I have found,
resides not only in what I pass through
but also in those
who pass through it with me.

As through a glass darkly

My clarity of vision
is not improved
by trying to see through lenses
clouded with all manner of grime.

Yet, this is exactly what I do
in so much of life.

I seek to know the world
through glasses begrimed by
prejudice, doubt, shame,
unrealistic expectations,
lack of hope, an inflated view
of my correctness in all things.

Awareness of this seems
especially important
with advancing age
when the need for aid
in seeing clearly
grows greater each day.

At a loss for…whatever

Every so often, someone's name
or the name of a flower or bird
slides into a dark pocket of my memory
where it nestles among loose coins,
car keys, lint.

Having taken up residence,
whatever its name
claims open-ended occupancy on its space
while evidencing great resistance
to ever being evicted.

There are times when the prodigal
emerges reluctantly,
though never sheepishly,
from its hiding place and,
on such occasions, desires no less
than a welcoming feast of fatted calf and fine wine.
Although I have yet to witness it openly,
I expect there is considerable envy among
those names that stayed home and at my service.

Should there be any hint of guilt over all this,
it seems I am the one to bear it
for misplacing the fool thing in the first place.

I have been assured this is not a sign of…
whichamacallit.

Backwater

Backwater.
Remote reaches of life
when we may not know where we are
or why we are
wherever we are.

Backwater.
Do people ever come here out of choice,
or is it a purgatory for unacknowledged sins
to which we have been assigned penance?

Backwater.
"The back of beyond,"
"middle of nowhere,"
"boondocks."

Backwater.
No address.
Unidentified on any map.
A GPS hostess announces only
that she is "recalculating."

Be hymns of peace with justice

Shout out in praise of empire
or sing glad hymns of peace.
Cry out in staunch allegiance
or sing songs of release.
The halls of power beckon
those who wish life to stay
within self-serving strictures
that mold our lives each day.

The empire prefers silence
o'er how it goes its way,
imprisoning detractors,
sequest'ring them away
in prisons dim and filthy,
where life is naught but pain.
The empire demands fealty
e'en when it's bought by chain.

The peace which empires offer
is by their conquests won
o'er all who would oppose them:
who'd see their might undone.
The antidote to empire
is through a people free
to seek a new equation:
that peace brings victory.

Be hymns of peace with justice.
Seek freedom for each life
that is oppressed by terror,
that knows only bleak strife.

Speak out against the powers
who work for naught but gain.
Lift high the flag of freedom
e'en if it threatens pain.

 Hymn tune: *Lancashire*

Building a packing list for the new year

What of past selves shall I carry with me
into the new year: into each new day?
As important, I suppose,
is what I elect to leave behind.

Surely, most of who I am, what I am,
will tag along with me, willingly or not, wanted or not
into the days and months ahead.

It is not easy, perhaps not even desirable,
to jettison too much of oneself too quickly
and run the risk of some form of identity shock.

The image of pruning seems an apt one:
remove redundancy, shape prudently
and pray that a new crop
has a chance of appearing this year.

One that will contain enough good fruit
to fill at least one pie.

Be the words you sing

Be the words you sing in worship.
Live the message they convey.
Let there be no breach in living
out Christ's message day by day.
Transform words into strong action,
turn intention into deed.
Live the trust which fires your spirit;
serve an earth in sorest need.

We are called to trust in power
though power's ends serve but itself.
Life is viewed as naught but resource:
gain its motive o'er all else.
We are called to challenge powers
who work evil on the earth
against brother, sister, all life,
leaving only death and dearth.

Let Christ's message fill our living;
may each action grow from love.
Turn life's rancor into concord
so we might hatred remove
between nations and their people,
between people and the earth.
May we act so each day's living
affirms every life's full worth.

Hymn tune: *Austrian Hymn*

Cautionary notes

The sign in a curio shop reads,
"Lovely to look at,
delightful to hold,
but, if you break it,
then it's sold."
A softer warning this
than the more menacing,
  "DO NOT TOUCH!"

With either declaration,
I know there are limits on my behavior
and should expect consequences
if I violate them.

What about those parts of life
which are not things at all,
such as other people?

I should not idly fondle
  another's source of pride
or pinch too tightly
  another's swelling bud of self worth.

Still, we do this with children,
and others with whom we claim close relationship,
usually prefacing our actions often nobly with
  "I am doing this for your own good."
or some other fictional explanation
  to justify ill-treatment.

Whose are they after we break them?

Contemplation

Presence of presence
without start or end,
no symbol captures,
no mind comprehends.
Source of all being
no name can confine.
Within around what is,
   you trace no line.

We for whom limits
shape the world we know
cannot conceive of that
which is not so.
Limitless, nameless
without place or time,
within, around all things
   complete, sublime.

Presence of presence,
without start or end,
no symbol captures,
nor mind comprehends.
We strain for meaning,
failing in our goal:
meaning of meaning,
   wholeness beyond whole.

Hymn tune: *Eventide*

Earth, the fruit of loving mother

Earth, the fruit of loving mother,
sing songs of joy.
Births all life as sister, brother,
sing songs of joy.
Nurtured, suckled at her bosom,
comforted by loving welcome,
we are born into her wisdom,
sing songs of joy.

She who stands astride creation,
sing songs of praise.
Is not owned by creed or nation,
sing songs of praise.
In her justice all things flourish;
at her breast all life is nourished.
Would that we would all life cherish,
sing songs of praise.

From her loins come all things living,
sing songs of love,
giving joy beyond believing,
sing songs of love.
With her breath she sets in motion
dashing clouds and crashing ocean.
Such a one deserves devotion,
sing songs of love.

In her wisdom all things prosper,
sing songs of joy.
when they heed her loving whisper,
sing songs of joy.

Heeding not the claims of nation,
giving all life equal station,
she would comfort all creation,
sing songs of joy.

Hymn tune: *Ar hyd y nos*

Candles

Perhaps I am part moth.
Candles fascinate me,
draw me to them.

I prize the single candle,
burning naked,
its flickers casting phantoms
on the wall.

Sometimes, I am tempted
to gaze steadily at the candle,
missing the effect it has
on the world around it.

Elderly

I would not describe myself as "elderly,"
though my age clearly places me
within the category used as a
shorthand reference for senescence
by younger reporters and broadcasters.

As in, "An elderly (man/woman)
was injured last evening...."
Sometimes, they include age
for clarity, but most often,
"elderly" is the sole identifier.

"Elder" is a term that carries
a positive connotation
when used about older people in many groups
around the world.
For generations, people have sought out elders
for counsel and approbation.
Some young even aspire to
become an elder of some kind.

I would prefer a report about me that begins
"A generously-experienced holder of great wisdom
and unparalleled humility...."

Spirit of the season 2012

Silent night, Sony night,
cyber gear left and right.
Frantic fingers race over the keys.
People shake and scream playing with Wiis.
There is no need for talking.
No need for talking at all.

Silent night, Microsoft night,
in their rooms out of sight,
family members with all kinds of apps.
Even grandpa's forsaken his naps.
There is no need for talking.
No need for talking at all.

Silent night, Apple night,
servers hum, no wires in sight.
Cyber beams running every device
for all children both naughty and nice.
There is no need for talking.
No need for talking at all.

Silent night, Amazon night,
Santa's gifts rated in bytes.
Eyes aglow in the light of a screen.
Christmas dinner by now turning green.
There is no need for talking.
No need for talking at all.

Waken to each moment's wonder

Waken to each moment's wonder,
to its fullness, to its grace.
Pause to sense its pregnant presence
before passing on apace.
Each new moment comes as vineyard,
vines full-laden with ripe yield.
Every fruit a fresh creation
from which new wine is revealed.

Waken to each moment's wonder,
enter ready to behold
what has ne'er before existed:
what has ne'er before been told.
Each new moment comes as vineyard,
vines full-laden with ripe yield.
Every fruit a fresh creation
from which new wine is revealed.

Waken to each moment's wonder,
plumb dimensions manifold
beyond those by spirit savored:
past what single heart can hold
Each new moment comes as vineyard,
vines full-laden with ripe yield.
Every fruit a fresh creation
from which new wine is revealed.

Hymn tune: *Beach spring*

When will we with wonder welcome

When will we with wonder welcome
all that life holds in its store?
When will we live out full sharing
using what we need, no more.
We are part of one grand union
spread throughout this fragile earth.
All life warrants its full measure,
no life holding greater worth.

Seen and unseen, life abounding,
we view all through minute frame.
Our lives rest upon the unseen,
rest upon life without name.
We are part of one grand union
spread throughout this fragile earth.
All life warrants its full measure,
no life holding greater worth.

When will humankind acknowledge
that all life is of one piece
and that all parts work together
or all life will one day cease.
We are part of one grand union
spread throughout this fragile earth.
All life warrants its full measure,
no life holding greater worth.

Hymn tune: *Austrian hymn*

Ancient pulses set life's measure

Ancient pulses set life's measure:
rhythms we dare not despise.
Seed must die that grass may flourish;
bulb must burst so stalk can rise.

Some yearn for a resurrection
to extend their length of days
into an eternal future
freed from life's pain and malaise.

All life presses for expression
in its own, evolving way.
Let us witness resurrection
in all things: in each new day.

We are prone to fret our ending:
ending we regard with awe,
thinking we deserve a future
somewhere beyond that of straw.

Yet the fate we deem our portion
we'd not share with all who live
but with only those whose virtues
parallel what we believe.

Who are we to parcel blessing
given our propensity
to view God through narrowed lenses,
not in God's immensity?

Astrophysics comes home

I swear that
our home is filled with black holes:
gaps in the fabric of the universe
where matter and light enter
seeming never to escape.

This seems a particularly cogent way
of explaining my frequent
loss of pens, datebooks, cameras,
special tools I need for special jobs
which, without said tools,
remain forever undone.

Certainly, this also explains so well
mysterious disappearances
of candy, given or received, and
remains of cake and pie
left after guests have gone home.

Perhaps I should begin immediately
to pen a treatise on this phenomenon:
one that will satisfy my wife's doubts
about the tenability of my explanations.

I must begin immediately lest I disappear
before I finish.... Now,
where did my notes go?

Autumn falls

Summer's end is close at hand
with autumn attempting to take the stage prematurely.
Canada Geese filled a nearby field last Tuesday,
although they are just passers through
on their southern migration.

Snow Geese and Trumpeter Swans
will make their appearance on Fir Island
in another month or so,
remaining with us until late winter
before returning north.

Days grow cooler, nights cooler still.
It's time to rummage about to find
a pair of flannel pajamas buried in a bottom drawer.
A closet holds flannel shirts,
the kind good for both indoor and outdoor wear.

Autumn is not a signal for us
to head for warmer climes.
Fall and the coming winter
lend variety to the world around us.
Some birds migrate south,
leaving the feeders to those who will winter over.
Leaves display a brilliance camouflaged in summer.
Deer exchange taupe coats for a darker covering.

As one in the autumn of life, I treasure fall's coming,
even as I acknowledge that winter stands in the wings
awaiting a cue for its entry.

Batter up!

Any pitcher worth his or her salt
comes to the mound
with a whole armload of pitches
to launch at waiting batters.

Fast balls, sliders, sinkers,
the good old "knuckleball,"
and, perhaps hardest for me to hit,
a fast-breaking curve ball.

Life can have this potential for us
as we expect it to dish up one thing
only to find what is hurtling at us
is far, far different from what we anticipate.

Batters, pitcher too,
succeed or fail based on their
expectations of what one another will do.

Never much of a hitter
against any kind of pitch,
I always prayed for something
I could see, estimate its speed, and
connect with.

I walked off my last diamond
several decades ago,
perhaps with my bat scoring a trail
in the dirt behind me.

Who knows how many innings
remain in my life: how many pitches
have yet to be hurled my way.

I harbor no illusions about hitting every one,
let alone connecting for a homerun.

What I need to do is to enjoy the game,
realize I am not the only one playing,
and be able to laugh, at least smile,
when my swing connects with nothing
but air.

Life's cup

Most days, my cup stands full,
some days running over.
Full of the love of family and friends,
of the beauty of earth in her countless expressions,
of shelter, food, health.

Perhaps I live the life of a fool,
for most of what I experience is blessing,
when this is not the case for countless,
perhaps most individuals, inhabiting earth:
those for whom life is nothing but a surfeit of bane.

Since neither their cup nor mine can be taken as due,
it gives me pause to think their cup as easily
could be my own.

C-a-w

Crows converse in nearby trees
on lawns, atop ridges of neighboring roofs.
Although I hear them,
there is little profit in
paying close attention,
for crow is one of a multitude
of life's languages
I do not understand.

There seems so much alike
in their utterances,
I marvel at one crow's ability
to decipher meanings
in the raucous noise of another.

Are there crows
with a reputation
for cawing too much?
For dominating
every exchange that takes place
when crows gather to natter?

That last call sounded
like a raven's guttural chuckle.
Perhaps raven, too,
has tired of the incessant
jabber of its smaller neighbors in black.

Then, its own reputation gives it little
to complain about.

Changing channels

Where amid the din of daily fare
can I find time, space
to hear melodies and rhythms
life offers in abundance.

What do I need to turn off,
turn on, to perceive life's music
in bird song, forest whisper,
the sound of my own footfall along a wooded path?

When will I pause to listen to my own breath,
messages of my own body
as it carries on in my behalf?

When can I listen without use of ears
relying instead on a ready, open spirit?

How long will it take me to wean myself
from incessant noise to which I have become inured
so I can turn instead to the gifts awaiting me
within its absence?

Cold days

Cold days.

Days where cold
seeps into every crevice
ignoring extra layers of clothing
and tightly stuffed insulation
to stab flesh,
chill bones,
render fingers and toes without feeling.

Days where chill
follows a body indoors
taking leave only in its own time.

Days where closet choices
tend more toward warmth
than fashion.

Days where the cautious of step
walk warily in a constant lookout
for icy patches.

Days where the reasons for curling up
with a good book are self-evident,
need no explanation to anyone.

Down sizing

The most recent fad to hit our fad-crazed nation
is downsizing to get rid of whatever it is
that clutters our lives: those things that, in many cases,
migrate to small, over-stuffed rental units.

My contribution to the downsizing effort
will be to reduce the collection of unused words
I keep on hand in "You never know when..." readiness.

The words I have in mind are ones
that turn tail, run, and duck when I look for them.
Perhaps they hide behind synonyms
or tuck themselves beneath an agreeable antonym.

These are words authors
insert into a piece of writing, often in italics,
that send the reader to the dictionary to find what,
if anything, they have to do with the story.

From here on, I'm going to keep at hand
only words of purpose: words I can pull up immediately
without an embarrassing...pause.
They will be words as familiar as my...name

A question I face in this effort
is where I should put words for which
I no longer have any use?
There is nothing I can see
to suggest there exists a market in used words
even though they may still have a fraction
of good tread left on them.

Is there recycling potential just
for the letters that make up the word?
Surely, letters from one word
can be used in another. Better yet,
perhaps they can be placed into the new words
that worm their way into new editions
of the Merriam Webster Dictionary
just because people use them a lot now.

Can I bequeath words to our children?
What happens to the words I still claim when I die?
Is this something else I need to discuss with our attorney
as an item for my will?

Beginning now, I will begin
stuffing words in the crevasses of theater seats,
leave them in the ashtrays of friends' cars,
scrawl them on restroom walls,
roll them in spit-wad size balls and flick
them during church services
at parishioners dozing during the sermon.

Ah ha! I'll employ them all in this year's
Christmas epistle. Watch for it!

Enlightenment pursued

The mysteries in which we dwell
stir questions oft ill-framed
about the ways all this began:
before the first bore name.
Each answer spawns more questions still;
some fear we search in vain.
Yet, quest is what we're embarked upon:
let not our fears constrain.

We quail before the magnitude
of what before us spreads
in cosmic grandeur without end,
in subatomic threads.
We build machines to stretch our reach
into the grand, the small
as we dwell, guests upon our home:
an ancient, fragile ball.

Our search will never be complete,
for newness will remain
beyond what human mind can ken,
beyond all known's terrain.
Our task is not to know all truth,
as if we would be gods
but rather to discern our place
upon this earth we trod.

Hymn tune: *Kingsfold*

Forward march

Rows and columns of teenagers,
instruments at rest,
pace back and forth
along the street behind the middle school.
No tattoo by a drum line sets their pace,
only the director's clapping hands
and shouted instructions.

"Keep the rows straight.
Stay three paces behind the row in front."
Oh, the burden that falls on the player
who sets the spacing at the right end of each row.
"Use your peripheral vision to keep in line,"
calls the teacher.
"What's a peripheral, teacher?"
Pray we don't hear, "What's vision?"

No drum major whistles signals
while wielding a long truncheon.
No high-stepping majorettes twirl, toss,
sometimes drop, batons
that grow slippery in rain, freezing in winter.
Today, a row of flutes leads the charge.

On the teacher's cue,
instruments are raised to playing position
but remain mute.
Drat, that's why I walked over:
to hear them play.

Nearly sixty years of memories creep out
of dusty music cubbies. Memories of marching,
keeping watch with my peripheral vision,
listening for the beat,
hefting my sousaphone to my right shoulder
while trying to read bouncing music.
All this for football game half-time routines
and multiple parades along Portland streets.

These years, I would need to be a four-armed Vishnu:
two to balance and play my horn,
a third to hold the walking stick I use
to keep from veering off track, and
a fourth to wave to my admiring public.

An irksome state

Each day, more and more people
attempt to live their lives
beyond my benevolent control.

What ingratitude they display
trusting in their own agency
to live fruitful, satisfying lives.

Next time they pray for my aid,
I'll ignore them.

Holy whispers

For the ordination of Sally Godard, M.D., M.Div., into Ecumenical Ministries of Justice and Advocacy of the United Church of Christ (Congregational), September 18, 2011, McMinnville, Oregon

Holy whispers clutch after our attention,
cause us to cup the ear of our spirits to hear,
perhaps even understand them.

But their importance rests not so much in understanding
but in their ability to jar us out of our too-familiar pursuits:
to release us from inuring patterns of everydayness.

Holy whispers, not quite voices,
or perhaps they are,
beckon us beyond ourselves.

They ready us for what could be
but only if we respond:
respond without needing a guarantee
of what lies ahead.

Holy whispers invite us to redirect our steps,
our lives, our souls
so that we might draw closer
to their sacred source.

How do our symbols limit faith

How do our symbols limit faith,
constrain our sense of awe
as we move toward life's sacred core:
as toward the all we draw?

As nails seal fast the coffin's lid,
symbols hold back our hope
by cutting short sacred's expanse,
delimiting faith's scope.

How can we all symbols exceed
to grasp the holy fresh?
How can we language supersede
with which we God enmesh?

We hear, we think we see the world
with symbols as our frame.
Oh, let us pause before we snare
sacred within a name.

Let me lend you a hand

There comes a stage, overnight it seems,
when aging parents are perceived by their children
as bordering on infirm. This is, of course,
not a perception shared by aging parents:
only by those they have birthed and reared.

At first, aging parents, may be disposed to bridle
at the prospect of being seen by their progeny as
less than able. They may resist,
even exhibit passive-aggressive behavior,
tantrums, or regress to more infantile
behavior, such as lapses in sphincter control.

The problem resides with us oldsters, however,
as we live to more and more advanced ages and
are subject to the vicissitudes of senescence.
If we abruptly stopped our exercise regimens,
went off the Mediterranean diet, began smoking,
and took up nude sky-diving,
many of these issues would resolve themselves.

Most old folk in my acquaintance are loath
to consider seriously leaving this mortal coil early.
That would deny them the pleasure
of watching their children struggle through
the teen years of their own offspring
or cause them to miss out
on one of the most important events of adult life:
their child's first colonoscopy.

Let peace peal forth with joyful cry

Let peace peal forth in joyful cry,
Send it resounding 'cross the sky.
Hate now resigns its evil day
As clouds of darkness pass away.
Let justice stir the chorus grand
Among all creatures, through all lands.

With shout of joy and thund'ring drum
Announce God's peace has now begun.
Ring out the bell, let trumpet sound
Proclaiming justice, too, abounds.
Set hearts aflame, let spirits soar
With knowledge we shall war no more.

Unfurl the banner, sound the call,
Set forth to carry peace to all.
Lift up the fearful, dry their tears,
Proclaim the peace of God is theirs.
Give voice to peace in grateful psalm,
Join hope to deed in healing balm.

God's peace appears too late for some
Who gave their lives that peace might come.
May they in sleep still share the day
When warring spirits pass away.
As on their shoulders we now stand
And sing out peace across the land.

Hymn tune: *Melita*

Living laboratories

Aging is a laboratory for
comparative anatomy and physiology
as we compare remaining body parts
to those we came equipped with
and how well these remaining parts work
in relation to how we remember
them working in earlier years.

Older friends of like age often gather
to compare observations,
discuss dietary changes required
by removal of one organ or another,
and share insights of the latest health guru
whose teachings they follow religiously,
at least until they happen upon a new guru.

Many losses result from our own
tom-foolishness and neglect. As to others,
it seems the scripture passage
dealing with the sins of fathers (mothers, too, I expect)
being visited on their children
are borne out via genetic transmission.

Why was so little of this information
offered in school curricula?
Was it an intrusion on family terrain
to presume to teach boys about the uterus
and girls about the prostate gland
(including how to pronounce it)?

Perhaps candles placed atop birthday cakes
should stand as memorials
to structures and functions
we no longer possess and carry on
with the obligatory singing of "Happy Birthday"
followed by a rousing chorus of
 "So long, it's been good to know you."

Observing my limits

Rocks sing and laugh
tickled by stream's frolicking flow.

Ancient evergreens gossip with one another
on the morning breeze,
nodding understanding,
shrugging in disbelief.
Side-looking birds chirp,
heads turning this way and that
to register their worlds.

I cannot detect the chatter of ants
as they labor in their nests,
or the fast-moving fid of the spider
as it mends broken strands in its net.

It is difficult enough for me to comprehend
that which my senses are attuned to take in.
Any more surely would overwhelm me.

Remembrance II

How abruptly life changes,
joggles and jumps so quickly
it leaves us breathless,
unable to feel
beyond grief's heavy ache.

We press to understand
  what is beyond
    all understanding:
yearn to know
  what we never can,
    never will,
      know.

Much we took for granted
to lend order to our lives
crumbled in an instant,
leaving behind only precious shards
  of what was, threads
  of what might have been.

The words, "How are you doing,"
are asked not so much out of curiosity
  as from caring.

They come now,
as they always will,
from love for us:
from a willingness to be part
of whatever form of
rekindled wholeness
we will one day
  know.

This moment I call life

This moment I call life,
this moment
  as ephemeral as sunlight
glinting off eddies
on a slow-winding stream,
is not something
for me to claim as due,
but to cherish
  as gift.

This moment I call life
  is too brief, too
    fleeting,
to reckon its consequence
amid the never-ending movement
  of moments.

Whenever, however
my moment ends,
may it,
in the timeless flow of eternity,
be judged to have lasted
  not a fraction too long.

To life in myriad, stunning forms

To life in myriad, stunning forms
arranged on sacred strand,
on which no life can by itself
assume that it will stand
alone outside the sisterhood
to which all life belongs;
it is to this variety
we lift our grateful song.

We label lives by well-set rules
that few can comprehend
then add on names for common folk
whose paths among them wend.
May we not let our names disjoin
life's continuity
as life flows into endless life
in perpetuity.

A single, animating breath
stirs all life to come forth
upon a fragile scaffolding
where every life has worth.
Our lives exist in common frame
with all life everywhere.
It is to this great commonness
we lift our grateful prayer.

Hymn tune: *Ellacombe*

Too soon old

This past January, I turned 75.
It seems to me
a man ought to know certain things
by the time
he reaches such an advanced age,
although such a list surely is not exclusive to men.

For example,
how full should I pour a guest's cup or glass?
Should I offer sugar and cream
or wait for my guest to ask?

Do I need to pass both salt and pepper
when a guest asks for one or the other?

Should a kiss on a woman's cheek
really be a kiss
or just a brush as I kiss air?

How about kissing a woman's hand?
Do my lips touch flesh then?
Should I worry about where her hand has been?

At what age do I need to stop standing
when a woman enters the room?
(At what age should I have started?)
Does my answer depend on which chair I select
on entering?

At what point in a visit is it acceptable
to ask to use a host's bathroom?
At what point is it too late?

If I buy a first round of beverages,
should I delay ordering a second
until my companion offers to buy?

What is an acceptable period
to wait for a companion at a restaurant
before ordering my meal?

What is an acceptable period to wait
before calling to see if I have the right day,
the correct restaurant?

Perhaps all this will come to me in an epiphany at 76.
But if it doesn't?

Valentine's Day 2012

This is the time of year when, as a child,
my hands started perspiring over the
annual prospect of having to create a
heart-shaped valentine with scissors
obviously designed by and for right-handers.

As a result of this experiment in social engineering,
I never learned to operate scissors with my
left hand. Who knows what other residual warping
shaped my life.

Anyway, the big white box placed prominently
on the teacher's desk elicited a Pavlovian response,
only perspiring instead of salivating.
Perhaps that, too,
but I was too busy drying my hands to notice.

I like to think that my difficulty in executing
a smoothly-curved, symmetric heart
was, in fact, a prescient understanding of
what the muscle really looks like
as it lub-dups its life-giving task
nestled in the chest cavity.

I also like to think it was
a southpaw entrepreneur who produced the first
pre-shaped, colored valentines
with faces and sappy sayings.
Lefty-or not, I salute such brilliance.

Some people are able to produce readily
anatomically-incorrect hearts they can present
to someone who either does not know
the real shape of the heart
or is too infatuated with the giver to care.

I, on the other hand, prefer to spend my time
browsing the card aisle to find a valentine
that approximates in word and image
my eternal undying love and devotion
without costing an arm and a leg, to say nothing
of costing a heart.

If you wanted, perhaps even expected,
a smoothed, symmetric greeting
from me this year, you can stop waiting.
This is what it is.
Happy Valentine's Day.

Now, excuse me. while I go dry my hands.

A trust large enough

As travelers on this tiny bark,
we sail an endless sea
that keeps expanding without end
through all eternity.

How does such grandeur shape a faith
that can all this enfold?
What sacred stories must we write
to all this wonder hold.

The countless stars beyond our own,
great galaxies that sow
new stars from out their fiery mass
beyond what we will know.

Is faith meant to enwrap all this
or work with smaller frame?
Still, we presume to capture all
within a single name.

Hymn tune: *St. Anne*

Among giants

Living close to towering white firs as we do,
I am drawn to their vigorous movements
when bullied about by the wind.
Barely have they recovered
from one hefty blow
before they are battered
by another,
then another.

They are marvels of flexibility
from base to tip.
Oh, they will fall,
do fall.
Some will be removed for safety reasons
by those who choose to live too close by.
Others, most I hope, will remain
until the work of age
weakens their massive root systems.

Our walks through the woods
sometimes take us
by a giant root system torn from the soil.
Like an octopus, its massive tentacles
extend in all directions.

"Board feet" constitutes the primary appraisal
of those who produce lumber from these giants.
For me, their real value rests
in their majesty standing erect, tall,
sheltering all manner of living things.
The last, a task they continue beyond death.

Boundary

I move amid hushed rustles
   of lives past.
Hardly whispers,
their stirrings more felt
   than heard.

Beneath the threshold of awareness,
they make their attendance known
in inchoate ways;
my understanding less important than
   just sensing their presence.

The boundary between life
and whatever follows life
grows less distinct
   with age.

God within me, God around me

God within me, God around me,
let me know that we are one.
Stir my actions, guide my pathways
'til my days on earth are done.
Help me press toward full completeness
in this time I walk the earth.

And when walking days are ended,
let my spirit know new birth.

From the morning of creation
you have dwelt among, within
all that your hand set in motion,
all that your love cast as kin.
There are ties which bind together
all that was, that is, will be.
Help me not in fragile moments
sunder that great unity.

As I pray, you stir within me,
as I pray, your love enfolds.
There's no sense of far off presence
But of one which gently holds.
God within me, God around me
may our prayer be unison.
Draw me forward toward completeness,
where in you all things are one.

In each aspect of creation
your expression shines anew.
Seekers follow different pathways
on their ways to finding you.
You in all things, all within you,
you the source, the way, the goal.
May your loving presence in me
fit me for a grander whole.

Hymn text: *Beach spring*

One benefit of growing older

Life has grown more precious
with the passing of years.
Not just my own life,
but all life about me
in whatever forms it takes.

Perhaps this sweet awareness
of life's variety and abundance
is common to older people
whose occasions for tasting it
grow fewer in number.

Many of us view life too narrowly:
a circle drawn
with the point of our compass
set too close to an increasingly
dull pencil.

"Hubbled" hubris

Piggy-backed on Hubble's shoulders,
we glimpse for the first time
stars birthed, dying and dead
eons before earth came into being.

Ignoring that we are but a fleck
in the gargantuan vastness of the cosmos,
we assign ourselves immense worth,
proclaiming we alone
are the universe's only singers
of an intelligent song.

Puzzlement

Last time I looked,
there appeared to be plenty.
   Certainly all I would ever need.
Now, when I look,
   none remains.

Where did it all go?
Such things don't just disappear
   without cause.

It's worrisome not having any left.
Unsettling, not knowing
where it all went
   so quickly.

The datebook

On the desk to my left, lies my datebook
filled with scribbles indicating all manner of events.
Some have been entered and crossed out.
Others have been scribbled in margins,
squeezed into corners of pages.

All of this is decipherable only to me
but not out of a need for secrecy of any kind.
The whole enterprise is intended to confer upon me
a fictive cloak of order as I enter a new day,
a new week.

It affords me the illusion I will not walk naked
into the future.

Hints of what is ahead

Is it a harbinger of autumn
that this August evening is cooling
so quickly?

Here and there,
maples sample colors
for their fall wardrobe.
Annuals turn brown from day-time heat and
the natural span of their lives.

Somehow, all this feels to occur
to a familiar, reassuring
cadence.

Got five minutes?

It seemed to happen most often
when I was relaxing in our small living room
that dad would stick his head in and
ask, "Got five minutes?"

Even though I probably wasn't doing
anything important or worthwhile,
I greeted his inquiries with
a measure of apprehension.

Typically, the five minutes of his request
would stretch into something much longer
and would involve working with him
in the garage or basement.

Whether he enjoyed it or not,
dad worked on our cars and
was usually able to identify and fix
whatever problem had arisen.

Sometimes, our five minutes would include
a trip to Tiny's wrecking yard on 82nd,
about a mile away.

Tinys' was a mausoleum for wrecked autos
and trucks, a large number of which
had sacrificed parts for other people's
weekend projects.

We might be in search of a generator
or some more esoteric automotive organ,

but Tiny always seemed to have one on hand
and, more surprisingly, knew where to locate it
among the wreckage.

For a lad growing up Baptist,
these trips to the wreckers often turned into
a seminar in obscenities and lascivious remarks,
all of which seemed quite fitting for a dark,
smelly office whose only wall decoration
was a calendar featuring a mostly-unclad,
attractive young woman.

By the time we diagnosed, secured the part,
drove home, and completed the transplant,
the "five minute" task stretched into a span
which must have been far longer.

Oh, to have a few more of those five minutes
now.

Hasta luego

I am of an age where hellos are precious
and goodbyes increasingly are
tinged with a measure of apprehension.

As I get older (and older still),
I become more aware
of the fact that life
does not continue forever, and
we may never meet like this again.
 Ever.

As much as it may seem like one, this
is not a source a despondency,
so much as it is a reminder
that I must treasure this moment
   with this person
   as fully as I am able.

I must stretch this moment

Time is too short for me
to view all of earth's wonders,
savor the fruit of every vineyard,
bask in the redolence
of every flowering garden.

Time is too short for me
to follow every path
winding among the trees,
marvel at the majesty of every soaring eagle,
taste the salty spray of every wave
that crashes upon the shore,
pause to scratch the ears of every dog I greet.

But there is still time
to gather friends in warm embraces,
whisper words of affection to those I love,
offer thanks for knowing the love
of the woman who most has given my life meaning
for over fifty years.

I must stretch this moment to its fullest
to experience as much of life's treasure
as I can.

Listen up, now!

Deep, penetrating bass horns
shout out the passage
of ferries and larger ships
on Guemes Channel beyond the hill.

Are there vessels still equipped
with brass bells rung
when weather closes in?
When visibility ends but a few yards
beyond the bow?

Mariners still need good ears
to maneuver through fog
notwithstanding the presence of radar
on even small craft.

There is such regularity
to the grand utterances of ships
these likely are controlled electronically.

Even so,
I fantasize about standing in the bow of my life
activating my horn
so the world will take note of my presence.

Then, perhaps this is ostentatious
   on a rowboat.

Olympics nostalgia

I grew nostalgic viewing the swimming events
at the London Olympics,
"I could do that," I thought.
Well, not now, of course.
Perhaps in another lifetime:
someone else's lifetime.

I thought back on standing in line
at the Portland YMCA
waiting for swimming lessons to begin.
All the boys wore the same outfit: nudity.
All of us naked newts queued
in the chlorine saturated air
to tromp through the foot bath
on our way to the pool.

Then there was swimming class in college.
I wore a swimming suit then,
but it didn't help me swim any better.

Later, I took lessons
at Blue Lake Park east of Portland.
That was less a swimming course
than one in humility.
If memory serves me correctly,
I dropped back a class every day I attended.
Before the course ended,
I had sunk to a level just above sucker fish
and may even have been enlisted
as a drowning subject for the Lifesaving Class.

Now in my dotage, I am once again at the pool.
Still wear a suit. Still don't swim well.
For what we are doing, I don't have to.
Our emphasis is on exercising frames
grown stiff and worn with age, and, I expect,
from earlier efforts at trying to learn to swim.

On seeing granddaughter Madison's prom photos

I remember what it was like to realize
my daughters had become women.
Now the same thing has happened
with my granddaughters.

Life seems to be moving in a sprint.
Hopefully, not the final kick
of a distance race, for I am not trying
to beat anyone to the finish line.

Most of the time, I feel as though I
have a few more good laps in me
and am not alarmed when others speed past.
We run our own races.

One of those days

There are days
when thoughts don't line up straight.
Distractions abound and intrude easier, and
concentration requires more effort
than usual.

Fingers fumble and strike the wrong keys,
two or more strike keys at the same time,
leaving an indecipherable jumble on the page.

Sometimes, mid-morning coffee
clears my cortical circuits.
Today, however, seems like one
when confusion will persist all day.

As I think about it,
you and I shouldn't try to talk just now,
especially if you want what I say
to make sense.
   Any sense at all.

Maybe I am thinking about this backward.
Perhaps fogginess is my natural state
interrupted by rare moments of lucidity.

Pardon moi, who?

Every now an then,
my masochistic side prevails
and I look on the web
to find the origin and meaning
of the name Densley.

By now, I know full well
that it has never in history
been part of a top-10 list of names.
It's probably not even included
in a top ten thousand list.

No question: it's a distinctive name.
Many people, on hearing it,
say they like it. Still, I balked
at giving it to our son. Now,
I kind of wish I had included it,
perhaps as his middle name.

Most people have called me Denny,
usually mistaking this as
the abbreviation for Dennis,
since high school.
My mom always called me Densley,
as did my grandmother Mac.
In his later years, dad sometimes
called me Denny
What I am called
is a mixed bag among my other relatives.

So, what of it.

Densley is a name seldom known,
even more seldom used.
If you call "Densley" in a crowd,
I am apt to turn around.
As are Dennis, Denise, and Denzel.

May what we carry of the past

May what we carry of the past
be ember for a flame
that brings new hope for all the earth:
that will our rancor tame.

We strain with hatreds centuries old,
their sources often lost,
when we should proffer succor, balm
without regard to cost.

We use earth's bounty to wage wars
discounting sacrifice
for lives existing, lives to come
whose hope is forfeit, lost.

May we shape tools of lasting peace
that foster concord's course
among all life that dwells on earth,
eschewing acts of force.

Hymn tune: *St. Anne*

Pondering

Sometimes, I wonder about things.
Truth is, I wonder about things
most of the time.

Perhaps I always did wonder.
It certainly has been the case
as I try to visualize
the tape ending this sprint called life.
Yes, I wonder about that.

A person who sits around spending
a lot of time wondering
can be misunderstood:
taken for frittering away his time.

Perhaps, I should grow a beard and take up
pipe smoking.
Then, I could stroke my beard thoughtfully,
kill time filling, tamping, lighting,
refilling my pipe,
(with time out for scraping the bowl
before striking it repeatedly against my hand)
and only then answer,
"I puzzle about that a lot, too."

Or, I could take up writing,
but then people really would know
I'm killing time.

Still life. Really?

*Based on a photo taken of me
at the August 2012
McMullen family picnic.*

Who is the old geezer
trying unsuccessfully
to camouflage himself
behind a door-prize planter
filled with summer flowers?

Can it be? No! Certainly not!
But yes! It is an aged version
of the pubescent boy forced
as a child to pose for photographs
in grade and high school band uniforms
while holding a potted red geranium.

What on earth possessed photographers
to stage such a photo shoot?
What possessed the hapless subject
to allow himself to be treated thus
not just once,
but twice in his lifetime?

The first was a questionable use
of film.
The second, a dubious use
of digital memory.
Both, an unrecoverable moment in time.

This image stands
as a tribute to the minutia
that fill life's special moments.
Had the boy posed with his sousaphone
snaked around his body like a giant boa constrictor,
would such a photograph now be branded
child hornography?

O, mystery of mysteries

O, mystery of mysteries, O, light beyond light,
we press toward your wonder but fall back in fright.
O, marvel most splendid, could we but draw near
the manifold aspects through which you appear.

We'd tether your nature with images, names
but our frail inventions can you never frame.
We covet your presence, sing grand hymns of praise,
neglecting your nature will ever amaze.

O, well of creation, O, source of all hope,
with you as our beacon we've no need to grope,
for in all creation you ply your deft hand
to fashion, to nurture all things small and grand.

Hymn tune: *St. Denio*

Year-end recollections

As the year ends, memories seep
from the mire of my mind.

Ill-formed oddments at the start,
they are filtered,
shaped by their passage
through accretion of thoughts and images
accumulated over the year:
over a lifetime.

What offers itself as full-blown,
coherent memory
is a blend never before known:
never to be known again
in exactly this form

I suspect this may be a good thing.

From
Pieces of my mind
2013-2014

A signature event

In a blinding burst of insight,
I have come upon the reason
for my lack-luster life,
assuming it is the reason
and my life has indeed been lack-luster.

Those we celebrate are identifiable by a
distinctive signature.
Even those whose signature is little more
than a quavering line, are known
by their mark.

People pay large sums of money
for a scrap on which a notable signature appears.

For my entire life, my signature,
such as it is, has changed little
from my initial, frustrating efforts at cursive writing
in elementary school.
Even efforts to make it more
distinctive and authoritative
turned out to miss their mark.

Once, I had a stamp made
of one of my better efforts at a signature.
The stamp is long gone, but my memories of it
remain, for it, too, was poorly done
and ostentatious.
There just aren't all that many reasons
for employing a stamp in everyday correspondence.

So, here I am at 77, pondering
how to make my mark, literally,
as something that will follow me into history.
Perhaps just my initials, or only my first initial
will suffice impressed with a signet ring.

Pardon me while I search for a piece of paper
or a baseball
on which to practice.

Eagle eye

As I watch an eagle
turning several hundred feet above my head,
I wonder,
"Does the eagle ever watch the likes of me
hugging earth with every step and wonder
how it is I do not soar?"

Eagles soared across the sky
thousands of years before I made an appearance.
They will continue to soar
thousands of years after I take leave of earth.

Knowing this will happen,
I find my brief stay here to be more acceptable.

A small step toward world peace

One point of contention
between parents and their children
can arise when the latter feel the need to separate
one of the former from his or her car keys.

As a gesture to world peace,
I have, for the time being, sapped the energy
from this source of contention
by losing my keys.

Well, "losing" is charitable,
for I harbor the suspicion the keys may have been
lifted from my pocket by some
well-intentioned family member's sleight of hand.

This will explain why,
on the occasion of our next hug,
I might, with great affection, pat you down
to see whether I can return normalcy
to our parent-child relationships.

Advent 2013

For what do we await at Advent:
shepherds and magi knocking at our gate?
What if it is not shepherds or magi who knock
but neighbors who have fallen on hard times?

An image of Syrian refugees fleeing the revolution
showed a pregnant woman seated atop a donkey
as she was supported by two men,
one on either side of her.
"My, God," I thought, "yet another Mary
destined to give birth in a foreign land?"

How many times must we hear this story
before we comprehend that, yes,
we are to care for, care about
our sisters and brothers?

And what of the child she carries?
Will it survive birth? Will she?
If they do, what will happen to them?

An unwelcome thought intrudes:
in what ways am I a Herod?
In what ways do I resist even slightest change
in social, economic, religious structures
that assure me of my life of power and plenty?

I pray I would not put those who are helpless
to the sword.
But in what social and economic forms
do I wield a sword?

Are their outcomes really so different
from Herod's massacre?

May we hush the Christmas din
so we can hear weeping and groaning all around:
so we can respond to it in love.
Leave off with our relentless clamoring for more
to let others claim their share.

Do not presume it falls to us
to bring the Christ spirit to earth;
it is here now, waiting for us to release it.

But all the kids have one

I carry around three portable devices
to help me make it through the day: a pen,
a pocket calendar, and a cell phone
which only makes and receives calls.

That I need all of these, carries a
modicum of embarrassment when,
at a meeting, the date is set
for a next gathering or special event
and I am the only one sans device.
The only one who needs to borrow a pen
if I have forgotten mine.

Many folk in their mid-70's, as I am,
have upgraded (at least I know the lingo)
to a single device which is a momentary stage in
the sizzling evolution of portable
communication devices fueled by companies
whose primary mission is to keep people
on the edges of their chairs awaiting the next,
newest great offering.

I harbor a sense of pride in being a luddite
when it comes to a lot of modern technology
and even a sense of superiority over those
who sit across a nearby table from a companion
eyes down, feet tapping, fingers racing over a
miniscule keyboard as a stream of images
flashes across a tiny screen.
Even the arrival of food seems of little consequence.

Not only have multi-billion dollar firms
created these devices, they have,
more insidiously, infected people with the belief
that they need these machines for a complete life.

But, my smugness wanes as I consider
that I work here at my computer, listen for
Joyce's car to enter the garage assisted by
a garage-door opener, and wonder
how my pace maker is getting along.

Challenging the mountain

They climb over, slog through,
detritus of last weekend's collapse
of the mountain within whose shadow
many chose to live.

We see mountains as features of earth
possessing immutable permanency,
and, like rivers and seas
believe they will always
remain in bounds we assign to them.

We bandy about the term "hero."
The term fits well here for those who,
by virtue of duty assigned to their occupations,
undertake the gruesome task of searching,
and also to those who claim the task
from some higher sense of responsibility
to humankind.

They walk, at times stumbling,
in the slurry of mud left by the mountain
and deepened by recent rains.
Much of their path entails
sinking in mire, sometimes to their waists,
where they call for help to move on.

They have recovered a few souls
who survived the event,
and the remains of others
who succumbed to its smothering weight and
unimaginable power.

Events like landslides, floods, hurricanes,
tornadoes are indiscriminate killers
who reveal no partiality to age or position.

Those who follow their destruction
emerge from all quarters
drawn only by the awareness of need and
the calling to render aid.
Even when aid is so that
grieving loved ones can only offer last respects.

For some, the soil and rock in which
they are interred by chance
will be that which claims them forever.
Still, that claim is not accepted unchallenged
by those who labor to find them.

Counting candles

Days and years come,
pass in a journey we know as
  life.

It is a quirk of ours
that humans find it necessary
to mark the passage of what we call
  time.

We are those who struggle
to find when the cosmos began and,
from that, ascertain its age.

We are the ones who,
when we are able,
assign birthdates,
mark anniversaries,
calculate the length of a life
  that, as all things, ends.

Yet, our assigning age
does not reach back far enough,
does not take into account
the ancient elements of the stars
we carry in us from the birth
  of everything.

Dapping

A beach washed by calm water
is a perfect spot
for searching out smooth, flat stones
shaped as if created solely to fit snuggly
in the curve of a bent index finger.

An arm pulled slightly back and to the side
then drawn sharply forward
provides energy for my missile to fly,
striking the water at a flat angle before skipping
once,
  twice,
    three times, or more
across the water,
  each hop shorter,
    touching more heavily
      before it finally buries itself
 beneath the surface.

Such an exercise naturally lends itself
to competition among humans
as throwers strive
to best one another for distance, and
  number of skips.

Practiced, perhaps for as long as land
  has bordered water,
as long as humanoids have trod shorelines,
dapping has been a less dangerous contesting
than other activities humans have perfected
  to show superiority to one another.

Though not so often anymore,
I try to dap stones,
although, like many efforts in life now,
performance falls short
  of anticipation.

In such a case,
I usually refrain from blaming the rock
  for this disparity.

A hymn of departure

Our congregation dwindled in size to the point where we could no longer afford to maintain our eighty-plus-year-old building. This hymn and the one following were written to acknowledge that reality.

Oh, the hymns these walls have echoed,
joyous anthem, prayerful lay.
Walls within which lives have sought for
how they might their faith display.
This has been a place of challenge.
This has been a place of peace.
Through the decades lives have sought for
how each might God's love release.

Words cannot the holy capture,
walls cannot the sacred bind.
Holiness is ever gracing,
showing favor to no kind.
This has been a place of challenge.
This has been a place of peace.
Through the decades lives have sought for
how each might God's love release.

Walls do not make congregations,
such are formed of covenant.
Walls cannot achieve containment
of that which is immanent.
This has been a place of challenge.
This has been a place of peace.
Through the decades lives have sought for
how each might God's love release.

That which has herein found nurture
may it now be broadly cast.
Where it lights may each seed flourish
yielding new life that will last.
This has been a place of challenge.
This has been a place of peace.
Through the decades lives have sought for
how each might God's love release.

Hymn tune: *Austrian hymn*

Doors

Hinges on the doors of time,
if doors and hinges there be,
begin squeaking as we foresee a day
when Pilgrim will close its doors
at 2802 Commercial for the last time.

Our doors have kept in heat,
kept at bay winter cold,
have served as ports of entry for
newcomers and regulars,

have marked comings and goings for decades
but never, we hope,
have been barricades,
real or perceived,
for exclusion of anyone who wished to enter.

We speak of a church building as being
a house of God, but
who is it that hung the doors,
installed locks,
kept the keys.

We say God never closes a door
without opening a new door. Really?
Does God think in terms of doors?
Of opening or closing doors?

Or, are doors devices we employ for security?
From what?
From whom?

Perhaps whatever we do in the future
needs to take into account
that God's love observes no walls and, certainly,
has no need of doors to be
opened or closed
   ever again.

Beat it

The approaching sound of drums
even before the band comes into view
always thrills me.
Causes my eyes to mist.

Then, as one band passes,
drums of an oncoming band echo with those
preceding it in a wonderfully
arrhythmic clash of sound.

Drum lines are the current rage.
I enjoy them, but
I miss the blast of the drum major's whistle
sounding its shrill signal to raise instruments
then listening for the drum pattern that precedes
the march's downbeat.

I miss it all
except for carrying my brass sousaphone
into the wind on a chilly fall day.

Every little breeze

Breezes have been scarce of late.
Where do they go when not about their task
of agitating shrubs and trees?
When not attempting to tear hats
from the heads that bear them or
turning umbrellas inside out or
relocating leaves from trees to lawn to curb?

Is there a meteorological black hole
that swallows breezes, winds, gales
when they are not working their bluster on us?

Of late, the absence of breezes and
their big sister the wind
has left us feeling our ways about
under an obstinate layer of fog.

Besides being gray and obscuring vision,
fog is damp, clingy, and, on occasion, a trifle eerie.
Grave yards are draped in fog.
Dense forests hang with sight-limiting murk.

Fog is not just a meteorological event but a metaphor
for our inability to grasp fully
the world about us: see with clarity
those who share the world with us.

Give us the hat-stealing wind,
the leaf-tossing gust,
the house-shuddering burst.

Get busy, wind, and sweep away
that which blinds us, chills us,
causes us to tremble with disquiet.

Life incomplete

To Erin

Wounds
sometimes appear as ragged holes
in the fabric of life
remaining after loss of one we loved.

Perhaps they did not know
their absence would leave
such a gaping hole.

Perhaps they might even have thought
they would not be missed at all.

Yet, they have.

They are.

A life that ends too soon
is a message interrupted.

Whatever additional meanings
there might have been

 we will never learn.

Gone but not forgotten, I think

Has anyone seen my 2013 pocket calendar?
You know,
the black one with non-standard issue gray duct tape
binding it together since the staples pulled through.

After repeated shorter absences,
my external memory for daily events
has really gone AWOL this time.

I have never been a neat writer or precise recorder
of the miscellany of my life.
If found, my calendar, wherever it is,
would provide stark evidence of this.

Scribbles, cross outs, arrows, abbreviations
(whose meanings are known only to me and the NSA)
fill the pages over and around coffee stains
and smudges of things I recall nothing about.

Was it that I bought a 2014 calendar a month or so ago
and began entering commitments for the new year
that sent 2013 over the wall?
Was it that it knew Joyce and I would be gone
at the end of the year and
had no celebration planned for it?

I am blaming the victim, aren't I?
It was I who lost my daily companion,
my confidant, my cognitive prosthesis.
Already, I am suffering from its absence,
and at such a busy time of the year.

Is there any consolation to be had?
Well, yes, if I make it to Thursday morning
when we fly south for Christmas.

Even today, even at this moment,
there may be some critical event taking place:
an event at which I was to make a report,
bring an address, or receive an award
for one thing or another, like memory prowess.

Permanency reconsidered

When I was a child,
and probably for quite a while after,
I attached permanency
to all elements of my life: oceans,
mountains, forests, people, pets.
What I knew had always been:
    would always be.

I'm not sure when the invalidity and impracticality
of this view struck me.
Perhaps it began with the death of
grandparents, pets, classmates
and such events as landslides and
    volcanic eruptions.

Still, underlying all of this,
was a belief in the permanency of myself:
> I would always be.

Long before the time I reached my present age of 78,
too much had taken place in my world
that put the lie to my childhood naïveté.
> And it keeps happening.

I no longer believe in a bedrock of certainty:
there's been too much death,
too much wanton destruction of earth,
too much willingness to cast aside what I had considered
> to be verities of existence.

All now leads me to mine the deep treasures to be found
in those with whom I share life each day,
to examine closely the panoply of life in all its forms,
to look at mountains and rivers as momentary expressions
of earth's ancient history,
to consider the cosmos still incomplete
as it presses
> to grow in its incomprehensible size and
> complexity.

I take less for granted in these years
that mark the final segment of my life,
for nothing lasts forever,
> including me.

Here's to the aging brain

Today, as I do every day,
I lug around an ever-shrinking brain
cradled in a bony, fluid-filled vessel
balanced atop my cervical spine.

Possessing an aging brain is, at best,
interesting. Sometimes,
it is anything but interesting.
Many times, it is downright inconvenient.

Aging brains,
though perhaps I am alone in this,
seem not to work with the speed
we think they once possessed.

Oh, they may never have fired with lightning speed, but,
because our brains are aging,
we do not recall this detail.

So far, I have yet to awaken in the morning
not remembering my own name
or that of the woman nestled in bed next to me.

It's not clear which forgetting
would be the greater problem,
not knowing my own name or hers. But
I expect I would soon find out
since she has snuggled in place beside me
for 54 years.

In the name of conservation

I think writing should not begin
on a blank page
but on one at least half-filled
with notes and doodles to serve as tinder
to ignite any creative impulse that might
intrude itself upon me.

Starting, especially with no idea in mind,
is often difficult for me to do,
perhaps because of inertia,
as in "A muse at rest tends to stay at rest."

Or, perhaps because of the blinding whiteness
of the blank page.

Like spraying graffiti on a freshly-painted wall,
its emptiness is a deterrent to defacing it.

At this point in my life,
I no longer leave notes on restroom walls and
don't scratch others' telephone numbers
or pithy descriptions about their prowess
on the wall above the phone.

Henceforth,
I will begin writing on an already sullied page,
ignoring whatever distractions it holds
while risking that my cogent efforts may pale
in comparison with the page's previous content.

Whether I ever write anything again,
I will, at least, have "gone green."

Living with a beast

Our hound Davey
displays a behavioral peculiarity
born of ancient urges to
hunt prey and, once found,
ravage its flesh with gnawing,
tearing fierceness.

The closest Davey comes to this
in the course of his domesticated life
is to identify the sounds made
as the last towel is torn from
the exhausted roll of paper towels.

Grasping the spent core from our hand
with a set jaw, Dave wrestles it
to the floor where he proceeds
to do what his kind has done
generation upon generation.
Soon, what had been a tube
becomes a scene of soggy shreds
of varying sizes.

Finished, Davey leaves the remains
of his conquest strewn about
the site of his savagery
and trots obligingly into the bathroom
to have his teeth brushed.

Meanwhile,
we are left like hyenas and vultures
to clean up
what remains of the kill.

On nation blessing

"God bless America, land that I love."
I remember Kate Smith singing these words
and heard them again recently.
They stir us,
fill us with honor and pride.

What is our response when we hear someone
singing the equivalent of these words, as in
"God bless Canada, Mexico, Iran, Russia, China…?"

Are we comfortable with the prospect that the God
we petition to bless our nation
   might deign to bless other lands:
   people other than our own?

Should we expect God to bless America?
   All of America?
   Everything about America?
Are there aspects of America we can be sure God,
if God is in the nation-blessing business at all,
   would not bless?

If God blesses America, Mexico, Canada, Iran
and every other land,
what might this mean
for how nations treat one another?

Would God's blessing come without contingencies?
Do we sometimes play Jacob,
conniving to gain God's blessing
   at our hungry brother's expense?

Is God's blessing an affirmation for a nation
or hope
   for what a nation could be?

Push 'em back

A wind out of the north drives chill air
through layers of would-be-warm clothing
donned before we left the house.

This is the kind of wind we get
from Alaska or Fraser River Valley
where they load it with giant blocks of ice
before shipping it south.

It is the kind of weather that drives
scores of small birds,
even a starling or two,
to our seed and suet feeders.

An unsuccessful attempt
to walk around the block
ended short of our goal because of the cold.

Had we been younger…

There seem to be a lot of "had we been younger"
explanations these days.

Organ recital

I find it interesting when visiting my physician
to spend waiting time
looking at charts on his wall diagramming
systems of the human body. My body.

These comport closely to diagrams I studied
in college anatomy textbooks,
at least enough so that I can
begin to fathom their intricacies.
At the very least, I can still tell the brain
from the lower reach of the intestines,
although some people persist in confusing these for me.

While interesting, such charts at my advanced age
hold a daunting quality, reminding me
how much I depend on the precise, or nearly so,
workings of the parts pictured
as well as billions left out for simplicity.

I can see where organs and structures
with which I started life have been removed
and can identify parts I in no way
want to consider for removal.

Then there are the vestigial structures,
like the appendix, that no longer have
survival importance for our species.
It makes a body wonder
why we had them in the first place.

Are they like what happened when I was a boy
and took apart alarm clocks,
only to discover on reassembly
there were a lot of parts left over.
Sometimes, these reappeared in spring
when we worked up a flower bed for reseeding.

Problem solving for the aged

While trying to figure out things electronic,
such as televisions and computers,
it has, at very long last, dawned upon me that
such devices and I operate in different ways.

Last evening, having spent a short time during the day
browsing at a sea of new television sets
because ours was not working properly
(perhaps it was but I did not understand it),
I sat once again with remote devices in each hand
attempting to stumble on the method I used previously
to get the device to function.

At last it did, but did I congratulate myself?
No, I sat trying to figure out what I had done.

Joyce asked me what I had done.
Two words came from my lips, "Don't know."
Perhaps there was a third or fourth expletive,
but I don't remember that either.

So much of my life has been carried out
on a trial-and-error basis,
with the error side of the ledger seeming far fuller.

Did I arrive on earth accompanied by
an operator's manual which, early on,
I tore to pieces or used as a coloring book?
Did my parents or older brother discard any such
document lest I become too independent?

While not on the cusp of death, so far as I know,
I am moving along with an ever-shortening string
called life. Surely, by this time, there are
general principles I should have learned
to guide me through life's labyrinth.

Long ago, I learned never to click
on my computer's HELP button
since it is an acronym for
Hardly Ever Lessens Perplexities.

Some things are better done in the dark

Halloween creeps slowly, clumsily
out of a darkened pumpkin patch,
trailing dried, crackling stalks behind it while
struggling to see without eyes
yet to be carved into orange flesh.

Pumpkins destined to become jack-o-lanterns,
better yet pies,
know only that they must escape this place
where they were born and
matured into generous orbs filled with
slippery orange meat and
a host of white seeds.

Some find their way into yards,
onto lawns, even into houses
where they signal arrival of the harvest,
the impending invasion of zombies,
queens, space creatures, and humanoids
possessing super-humanoid powers.

They throng through neighborhoods
extorting payments of candy
in exchange for mischief.

Coward that I am,
I always accede to their threats.

Something's missing

Guemes Channel lies north just over the hill from us.
Although our sky may be sunny and clear on this side,
fog often settles in much of the day along the channel
obscuring boats, large and small,
from each other.

This is one of those days when ships,
especially the frequently-sailing state ferries,
announce their movement with basso profundo voices
that carry fortissimo over the hill.

When we moved here in 2001,
there was a horn that announced to mariners
the presence of Shannon Point,
a spur that runs into the channel
from the north side of Fidalgo Island.

It no longer sounds: hasn't for several years.
I suspect people who built farther north complained
about what they determined to be noise,
and the Coast Guard,
semper paratus, complied.

Those folk may live in bigger, newer houses
but appear to lack poetry in their hearts

Thin places

We try to build thin places
where God and life are met,
but such spaces are blessing,
and not by deft hand set.
It falls to us to know them
as we the sacred seek.
It falls to us to hear them
when to us sacred speaks.

It is the heart perceives them,
a spirit well attuned
to harmonies eternal
which through the ages croon.
It falls to us to know them
as we the sacred seek.
It falls to us to hear them
when to us sacred speaks.

I seek, in this brief moment,
a thinness to reveal
where temporal and sacred
unite, that I might heal.
It falls to us to know them
as we the sacred seek.
It falls to us to hear them
when to us sacred speaks.

Hymn tune: *Aurelia*

Too good to be true?

A pop-up ad on my computer announces
I can learn a language in ten days.
This surprises me since I have worked at
learning English for over 77 years
and still have considerable distance to go.

Early on, I learned not to end a sentence
with a proposition; they were not my school teachers
who taught me this rule
but my friends in the neighborhood.

The dissonance between who and whom continues,
although some propose solving the issue by
firing "whom." Or is it firing "who?"

Are those of us with partial colons
forever consigned to using semi-colons
and the fuss this requires in using them correctly?

None of these touch on the real
pachyderms in the room:
diminished vocabulary and proper word order.

I am more sensitive to this now that words
do not come as readily as I think they once did.

Living with this lack is easier since
so little comes as readily to mind.

Truth is where you find it

It is suggested by my children and wife
that I tend to manufacture explanations
from whole cloth.
Oh, I don't do this so much anymore
now that my credibility
has been so repeatedly and painfully disparaged.

What I remember mostly is that,
after offering what I thought to be a cogent explanation
of nature, people, all things ambiguous,
one of the children would stab me with the question,
"Is that true, mom?" No, they didn't ask me;
they asked their mother to confirm my veracity.

While my intent, and I just made this up,
was to teach them not to believe all they heard,
they were to be, like Sgt. Joe Friday of LAPD,
concerned with "…just the facts."

Perhaps it was this incessant questioning I endured
that led me to decline invitation after invitation
to write sections for Encyclopedia Britannica.
There is an aura of sureness, factualness,
indeed, dare I say it, truth attached to those who write
such entries and to the entries themselves.
I shunned such absoluteness.

BUT, and I hasten to point out,
how many times has E.B. had to be revised
because of inaccuracies or more recent discoveries?
Or because of the writer of an entry

turned out to be bonkers or an outright fraud?
Well, I don't know either, but it's
something to think about, isn't it?

Already, I hear in my mind,
a chorus of children's voices,
 seeking authority from their mother:
"Is that true, mom?"

Again, my soul shrivels a little.

Thanks an awful lot, God

Although I thank other people for their kind acts
and even thank our dog when he engages in
people-friendly behavior,

I think offering thanks to God for this, that,
and the other diminishes
the nature of the thanks we offer.

We are to be thankful in all things, not just
the ones we favor: the ones in our best interest.

But how, you ask, can we thank God
for loss of a loved one, disease, unmerciful acts
performed by others, unrelenting pain?

I don't know the answer to these questions,
but I suspect it resides somewhere at the very nub
of what the mystery of faith in God is about.

Veterans Day 2013

A reflection

We are given to glorifying the lives and deaths
of those we send
to wage our nation's battles.

We bandy about terms like
"bravery" and "hero"
as if these can salve our national conscience
when fighting men and women,
if they come back at all,
often return damaged beyond repair.

We send young people into places, scenes, actions
for which they are too young and inexperienced
to see friends and comrades blown to bits,
torn apart by bombs and shells, overwhelmed
as any of us would be overwhelmed,
by the constant din of explosions,
shouts of attack and groans of the dying.

No medal, no flag dipped to half staff, no bugle call,
no mellifluous patriotic speech or 21-gun salute
is sufficient recompense for our blatant disregard
of the value of life.

May we look upon our combat veterans
with deepened appreciation and closer scrutiny
at what we ask our young to sacrifice

When the mountain fell

There is so much we take for granted in life.
Mountains, rivers, seas, objects in space,
the wind are all assigned spaces in our worlds.
Spaces we expect they will fill in an orderly,
predictable manner.

Then, a mountain falls, as it did on March 21,
releasing tons of rubble
that obeyed only the laws of gravity and fluid dynamics.

That happened last Saturday,
when Skagway Mountain yielded
to its unstable soil, fractures and unrelenting rain
and slid to cover what lay beneath it:
nests and lairs, homes, trees, a highway, river, people.
A muddy slurry that flowed around, over, through
everything in its path.

There are those who seek to fix blame,
establish liability for the event and its consequences,
denying that nature does what nature does:
flood, crush, uproot, kill whatever is in its way.

We do not like to admit to our ultimate weakness,
to believe that we cannot control everything
once we put our minds to it, leaving us
to respond with grief, anger and, at rock bottom,
an overwhelming sense of impotency.

Pieces of my mind 2013-2014

From
And around we go
2014-2015

A less-than-sacred ritual

The annual rite of driving to the stationery store
to buy a new pocket calendar
takes place next week.

You know from other writings,
that I, in true luddite form,
carry a pocket calendar suitable
only for filling in appointments
while unequipped for taking photographs,
placing calls,
plotting my course to an unfamiliar destination,
or tracking some obscure aspect of my physiology.

Hurrah for those who are up to carrying
and using such devices,
except when they deploy them
at the coffee or lunch table.

As for me, I loathe holding anything in my hand
that outpaces my wit in ways I will never understand.
Perhaps with greater wit…

My major decision each year is to determine
what size and color book I will buy and carry with me
wherever I go: something that will
complement my drab apparel and
whatever suspenders I happen to wear that day.

Something that will look just as good when I apply a
gray, duct tape accent next July to hold it together.

And around we go

Does the old year step up its pace
as the end of earth's circuit around the sun
comes into view?

I read today that, since its discovery in 1930,
Pluto, planet or not,
has yet to complete its circuit of the sun
and will not do so until 2178.

Will it be met by an excited throng
to cheer it on its next orbit
in the way we do for earth
every 365 days, or thereabout?

Given human lifetimes, I estimate
we will have to replace ourselves
at least three times before Pluto
completes its loop.

The way humans treat one another,
as well as the earth,
                        that may be a stretch.

Best in show

As we finished breakfast this morning,
our conversation turned to the just-completed
NYC Westminster Dog Show.

Davey, curled in his bed by the table,
perked up at the word "dog" and asked,
"Didn't a pert little Beagle win Best in Show
this year?"

We think Davey has yet to forgive us
for not entering him among the canine contestants.

Truth be told, we let the date for the show
creep up on us undetected.
"Us" did not include Davey.

At nearly twelve years of age,
we concluded a few years ago
that Davey is past his prime for competitive showing.

Perhaps the error in our thinking
should have been obvious from Davey's
rapt attention to the images of Westminster.

There is next year, of course
and a lot of preparation for participation,
to say nothing of the exorbitant fees
levied on participants.

What we may do is to secrete Davey
into the stands where he can bark and bay

without fear of receiving a point deduction
and where he can distract contestants
at critical moments.

We can see the headline now:
"Geriatric hound wins Pest in Show."

Silent partner

While working in a front bed yesterday,
Joyce enjoyed the company of one of our
many neighborhood does.

According to Joyce,
neither of them tried to hold a conversation
with the other,
just enjoyed a silent time of being together.

Perhaps the deer is on the verge of delivering
a new fawn or two to augment the growing number
already added to the herd this year.

Perhaps the deer knows that Joyce delivered three new
lives and might have expert advice to share.

Perhaps it is that Joyce, a gentle person,
attracts other gentle creatures to share her world.

I like this explanation best.

Early morning wonder

When I let Davey outdoors
to attend to his morning needs,
I sometimes step onto the deck,
or at least lean my ear out the door
to hear the early sounds of birds as they awake
and offer their songs to the new day.

I delight in the variety of voices
calling from shrub and tree.
Do they tell of their dreams of the night,
their plans for the day,
or do they just sing because vocalizing
is what they do?

Are some voices warning others
to shut their beaks and go back to sleep?

Birds and their calls are, for me,
one of the new day's most beautiful gifts
no matter what they might be saying
to one another.

I am tempted to join them,
yet I expect the voices
I am likely to hear in return would
be telling me to pipe down and go back to bed.

When I think Davey has been out long enough,
I may whistle softly
or quietly call his name.
When he does not come promptly, I wonder whether
he, too, is listening to the birds.

Life needs an instruction book

Life is fragile,
brittle even,
as we try to respond to its unpredictability.

Others' lives,
our own,
often move in unforeseen,
sometimes unwelcome ways.

All this runs crosswise
to our penchant for linearity
and predictability,
our stretching after certainty
amid the flux of daily events
over which we have no control
despite our best intentions.

We can brood about this,
wish it were otherwise,
but without salutary effect.

One might think we would learn
this to be the case.

One might think…

And around we go 2014-2015

Once again into senescence

The vagaries of my aging memory
never cease to surprise and, yes,
frustrate me.

These include forgetting things I have known
to remembering those same things
at inappropriate times.

Recently, I developed a new list of return address labels.
They were quite nice,
featuring a holiday theme.

When it came time to enter names and address,
I typed in what had been the numbers of our address
in McMinnville 15 years ago.

We have already received a query
from one person who wondered about my error.
I hope there are others since
their lack may mean either they did not
note the problem or have taken an eraser
to their address books.

And around we go 2014-2015

Seeking the lost

Searching for what I have mislaid
consumes more and more of my time
when I have less and less time to waste.

At the moment, I am missing
our cell phone and my date book.
The likelihood of there being
other items among the lost
seems high these years.

I have rifled through the pockets of trousers,
patted down jackets, and probed vests
hanging in my closet, all for naught.

I have plumbed the depths of memory
for where I last had each one,
could have had it, perhaps
even should have had it. Again,
all for naught.

One would think that,
with two of us to mount a search,
we would increase our odds of success.
Not so.
Perhaps we increased the odds of success
but the missing remain missing.

There is always the last resort
of replacing phone and date book with new ones.
That method seems so… final.

Would you mind keeping an eye out
for a small, black "flip phone" and
a black vinyl covered datebook for the year…

I will leave the year on the book open ended
so you can assist me in the future, for, if nothing else,
I am a creature of habit.

By the way, this is the only apology
you will receive from me regarding
an unreturned telephone call or missed appointment.
Senescence is a harsh business.

Putting away Christmas

Into which box does Jesus go
when Christmas is over?

Each year, we take down ornaments
of the season on this day
that divides year from year.

Bows and decorations
assume their places in large boxes
to be stored on a shelf in the garage.

In which box shall we place Jesus?
Or, perhaps, in no box at all?

And around we go 2014-2015

Seeking the lost redux

The angels heard my cry and responded
with a batting average of .500.

Believing that prayer
must be accompanied by effort,
I drove to the local stationery store
and purchased a new pocket calendar
to replace the one I lost
and began making entries.

Our son-in-law Ray served as a divine
intermediary and found my cell phone
in a place both Joyce and I had searched.
I thanked Ray but, given his taciturn countenance,
refrained from embracing him and planting
kisses on each cheek.

The relief I felt after order was restored to my world
was palpable — at least to me.

Hurrah for sons-in-law who can find things
where the sun don't shine.
Hurrah for stationery stores who know enough
to stock more than just one date book.
Hurrah for the elements in all of this
of which I remain unaware.

Thanksgiving 2014

Now 'tis season for the harvest
of all that which earth provides.
May we share in her abundance
with all who on earth reside.
Lift glad hymns for all earth offers
as we share with all in need,
for earth's creatures share in common
thread from ancient, sacred seed.

We give thanks for all who labor
to bring in what we enjoy.
May we honor all their toiling:
man and woman, girl and boy.
Lift glad hymns for all earth offers
as we share with all in need,
for earth's creatures share in common
thread from ancient, sacred seed.

Let each new day bring thanksgiving
for what that day holds in store.
May we not let greed diminish
in our press for more and more.
Lift glad hymns for all earth offers
as we share with all in need,
all earth's creatures share in common
thread from ancient, sacred seed.

Hymn tune: *Austrian hymn*

Thanksgiving 2014 II

The fields are ripe for harvest;
their fruits are gathered in
against approaching winter
when fields will rest again.
From seed to bud to flower,
life toward fulfillment tends.
Likewise our paths are fashioned
from birth till each life ends.

Each life has destination
recorded in its seed,
though each step holds a myst'ry
disclosed as life has need.
From seed to bud to flower,
life toward fulfillment tends.
Likewise our paths are fashioned
from birth till each life ends.

We praise the one who made us,
who nurtures us with love
and sees us to fruition
as we throughout life move.
From seed to bud to flower,
life toward fulfillment tends.
Likewise our paths are fashioned
from birth till each life ends.

Hymn tune: *Aurelia*

On turning 78

A few days ago, I turned 78.

This is not a singular honor, of course,
since throughout history countless others
have turned 78 and older.
Even many among my friends now lay claim to this age
and beyond.

This is the first time for me.
The last, too, I expect.

So, 78.
Is there something special I am to accomplish
at age 78?
Clearly, there are many things
I should have accomplished by now.

Taking as my motto the words Shakespeare
assigned to Antonio in *The Tempest*,
 "What is past is prologue,"

To what is my past prologue?
In Antonio's case, he and Sebastian
were planning murder.
There is nothing to suggest
this is what my future holds.

So, as I embark on another year,
perhaps another decade,
I will scout out significance
in each moment.

The truth comes out

I don't recall what grade I was in
when a teacher taught me
how to outline
something I planned to write.

On and off through the years,
I have tried to use outlines
to lend coherence to my writing —
assuming it was something
about which coherence was required.

If I recall correctly,
the system alternated between
key points designated by Roman numerals.
These were to tell my reader that,
in this section, they were to pay attention
to my argument.

Next came lesser points that were,
I was advised,
to support what I had designated by
an upper case letter.
These lesser points were supposed to demarcate
paragraphs in my writing.

Then came subordinate items,
or were they insubordinate,
whose main purpose, as I understood it,
was to pad paragraphs full
of innumerable items of little importance
to much of anything.

These were designated by Arabic numerals.
I needed to have a passel of these
to convey a smidgeon
of understanding why I was writing the damned
thing in the first place.

Then came items of even lesser significance
identified by lower case letters.

From here on, I was to demonstrate
a tedious grasp of the topic
with a seemingly unending list of items
set off by letters and numbers
surrounded by parentheses,
the number of parentheses enclosing a number
or letter denoting points of lesser and lesser importance.

If I recall correctly, there was a time or two
when I wrote what I wanted to write
and constructed an outline that seemed to fit
and added it afterward

Teachers seemed to wise up to my option
by requiring me to turn in my outline
before I started my essay.

Then, they graded my outline and handed it back
to be corrected.
At some point in this give-and-take,
I was able finally to start writing in earnest.

But, by that time I had tired of the entire enterprise
and decided never to write again.

As you can plainly see.

And around we go 2014-2015

There went one now

Ideas flit through my mind
like questing humming birds,
and light, if they light at all,
for only a fraction of a moment.

It's not that I wish to perseverate on sterile thoughts
which only clutter the workings of my mind,
but I do wish that whatever nectar resides there
is at least sampled
and shared to pollinate others' ideas.

This difficulty of snaring and holding
a passing idea
has become more apparent in recent years

and is especially annoying
when it happens mid-conversation
leaving both me and my listener wondering
how my idea will turn out.

The most likely explanation,
most likely and most unpleasant to consider,
is that the fault resides in the slowed
functioning of my brain.

Should my insight be accurate,
it affords no comfort.
No comfort at all.

Who goes there?

The media announce more and more frequently
that one giant data system after another
has been hacked.

This causes me to wonder how it is
hackers can type their way into
supposedly secure systems
containing data on millions of people
they do not know,
when I cannot remember how to access
my few accounts.

From retirement accounts to health care systems,
I am unable to call up my user ID for each system,
my latest password, or even the answer to my
self-selected security question,
(when I can bring to mind the question).

To this point, my health records
and retirement accounts
have not, so far as I know,
been compromised by anyone.

The scramble of rumpled papers
on which I jotted access information
is devoid of anything useful —
at least from the snappish, red-accented messages
I receive from whatever system
I am laboring unsuccessfully to access.

And around we go 2014-2015

When these experiences pile on top of normal
day-to-day forgetfulness, I worry that I tread
the verge of being declared *non compos mentis*,
by those who store information about me--
as well by many others.

Should I worry that the Pearly Gates
will have access codes, require a password
assigned to me *in utero*, or want to know
my grandfather's maiden name?

My paramount mortal fear, however,
is that public restrooms will one day
install access systems that,
in my moment of urgent need,
refuse to identify me and allow me to pass
where I am supposed to pass.

I suppose that, were I as important
as I think myself to be,
I would have underlings to remember such
minutia of modern living.
All I would have to do
is recall their names.

Enough — a last offering

Enough.
I've written and said
enough over these past several years.
More than enough, I expect.

I have always thought it important
for a speaker or writer, to know
when enough is enough:
to know when to stop.

When I have experienced this in a presentation,
I have grown restless,
even angry that the speaker
drones on.

There comes a time for a person
to stand,
move toward the aisle while
taking care not to step on the toes
of those who either share a different view
or who are too timid
to use escape as relief for their pain.

But I drone on.
Enough.
Thank you for listening
over this past decade.

Do not be embarrassed to stand,
move toward the aisle.

Everyone is.
Race you to the door.

ALPHABETICAL LIST OF POEMS

A glorious morning breaks anew	45
A gradual healing	139
A hymn of departure	215
A less-than-sacred ritual	243
A richer walk	140
A signature event	205
A single candle	50
A small step toward world peace	207
A trust large enough	181
Advent 2013	208
Among giants	182
An irksome state	167
Ancient pulses set life's measure	155
And around we go	244
And did I tell you…?	86
And God divided light from darkness	27
And the greatest of these	87
Annual pruning	88
As old as the wind	90
As through a glass darkly	141
Astrophysics comes home	156
At a loss for… whatever	142
Attending to final details	28
Autumn falls	157
Autumn reflection	91
Backwater	143
Batter up!	158
Bay waters	92
Be hymns of peace with justice	144

Be the words you sing	146
Beach leavings	53
Beat it	218
Best in show	245
Birds of a feather	89
Boundary	183
Brass rings	29
Building a packing list for the new year	145
Busted	93
But all the kids have one	209
By what light do we guide our steps	81
Candles	150
Can't you understand anything	58
Casting the first stone	95
Cautionary notes	147
C-a-w	160
Challenging the mountain	211
Changing channels	161
Changing of the Guard	3
Choices	94
Christmas confession	95
Closeness	97
Cold days	162
Come and get it	97
Come together sing of oneness	5
Contemplation	148
Color crayons	99
Consolation	101
Conundrum	4
Counting candles	213
Dancing	7

Dapping	214
Do I really need this?	102
Doors	217
Down sizing	163
Each new morning is but moment	30
Eagle eye	206
Early morning wonder	247
Earth hymn	103
Earth, the fruit of loving mother	149
Easter 2010	32
Eddies	40
Eighty-eight names	104
Elderly	151
Encountering sacredness	105
End of year musing	106
Enlightenment pursued	165
Enough—a last offering	261
Every little breeze	219
Evolution at work	108
Exile	109
Fall gown	59
Fire song	31
For whom shall we strong voices raise	110
Forward march	166
Gestalt	33
Gestation	55
Getting in the word last	111
God within me, God around me	183
Gone but not forgotten, I think	221
Good company	112
Got five minutes?	188

Hasta luego	190
Here it is again	9
Here's to the aging brain	224
Hints of what is ahead	187
Holy whispers	168
How do our symbols limit faith	169
How memory works 101	60
How shall I sing when words won't come	11
How shall we behold the wonder	114
Hubble	34
"Hubbled" hubris	186
I lift a song with all about me	12
I'll be back with you in one moment	115
I must stretch this moment	191
In a word	117
In each of life's newborn moments	84
In the name of conservation	225
Infernal, internal switchboard	119
I would pluck splinters from your eyes	8
Images of ending	61
Join the dance into a future	107
Justa cuppa coffee	35
Kenosis	36
Knowing our place	13
Lamentation	74
Learning my place	37
Let each new day an advent be	83
Let me hear you	64
Let me lend you a hand	170
Let peace peal forth with joyful cry	171
Let the words of my mouth	85

Let us raise our hymns anew	133
Life incomplete	220
Life needs an instruction book	248
Life song	14
Life's course	120
Life's cup	159
Listen up, now!	192
Living laboratories	172
Living with a beast	226
May others sing our message	122
May what we carry of the past	197
Memorial	38
Misleading ourselves	57
Mistake making	123
Morning coffee	39
Morning comes naked	41
Mother's Day Hymn, May 9, 2010	62
Mystery	63
O, mystery of mysteries	200
Observing my limits	173
Of moments	42
Olympics nostalgia	193
On a rainy afternoon	64
On nation blessing	227
On seeing granddaughter Madison's prom photos	194
On turning 78	255
On wisdom	19
Once again into senescence	249
Once broken	125
One benefit of growing older	185

One of those days	195
Organ recital	229
Orienteering	126
Our children die	128
Pardon moi, who?	196
Permanency reconsidered	222
Pockets	43
Pondering	198
Porches	15
Prayer words	65
Problem solving for the aged	230
Pulses of life	124
Push 'em back	228
Putting away Christmas	251
Puzzlement	186
Remembrance	66
Remembrance II	174
Sacred space	54
Sacredness beyond illusion	44
Sanctuary	67
Seeker's lament	69
Seeking the lost	250
Seeking the lost redux	252
Silent partner	246
Sing of promise, sing of coming	82
So much for the old year	129
Some things are better done in the dark	232
Something's missing	233
Somewhere a bell is ringing	46
Sowing poems	71
Spirit of the season 2012	152

Squeezing life	72
Still life. Really?	199
Stream	47
Summer reflection	113
Swaddling sacredness	17
Sweet water	130
Tears to come	71
Thank you for listening	72
Thanks an awful lot, God	237
Thanksgiving 2009	73
Thanksgiving 2014	253
Thanksgiving 2014 II	254
That awkward stage—again	116
The datebook	187
The search for God	68
The truth comes out	256
The well	131
There be dragons	49
There went one now	258
Thin places	234
This moment I call life	175
Though I no longer walk among you	20
To life in myriad, stunning forms	176
To S	18
To sleep, perchance to dream	70
Too good to be true?	235
Too soon old	177
Truth is where you find it	236
Unending seeking	75
Valentine's Day 2012	179
Vanishing memory	75

Veterans Day 2013	238
Waken to each moment's wonder	153
Waking	76
Walking life	55
We are people of a journey	132
We come in our diversity	56
We do not kill	77
We drink of common water	52
We dwell at the margin of shore, sea and sky	6
We sing of a Presence beyond human ken	21
What we do for love	135
When we work for justice	48
When the mountain fell	239
When will we with wonder welcome	154
Where do I take this faith I claim	22
Where shall we sacred search today	23
Whittlin'	51
Who goes there?	259
Wind is forecast	76
Wisdom's candle	59
Word woman	136
Year-end recollections	202

About the author

Densley Palmer is a layman and retired psychologist and educator who shares life with Joyce Eileen Fields Palmer. Both Densley and Joyce were born and raised in Portland, Oregon, attended school together from elementary school through college, and have spent their married life moving between graduate study and jobs in Oregon and Washington while raising three (now adult) children. Densley retired from Linfield College in 1999 where he served for 16 years and was named Director of Counseling Services emeritus upon retirement. He and Joyce live in Anacortes, Washington.

August 2015

www.ingramcontent.com/pod-product-compliance
Lightning Source LLC
Chambersburg PA
CBHW070638050426
42451CB00008B/206